WORK, MANAGEMENT, AND THE BUSINESS OF LIVING

WORK, MANAGEMENT, AND THE BUSINESS OF LIVING

MONEIM EL-MELIGI

NEW JERSEY · LONDON · SINGAPORE · BEIJING · SHANGHAI · HONG KONG · TAIPEI · CHENNAI

Published by

World Scientific Publishing Co. Pte. Ltd.

5 Toh Tuck Link, Singapore 596224

USA office: 27 Warren Street, Suite 401-402, Hackensack, NJ 07601

UK office: 57 Shelton Street, Covent Garden, London WC2H 9HE

Library of Congress Cataloging-in-Publication Data
El-Meligi, A. Moneim, 1923–
　　Work, management, and the business of living / Moneim El-Meligi.
　　　p. cm.
　　Includes bibliographical references and index.
　　ISBN-13: 978-981-279-067-5 (alk. paper)
　　ISBN-10: 981-279-067-5 (alk. paper)
　　1. Management. 2. Leadership. I. Title.
　　HD31.E555 2012
　　658--dc23
　　　　　　　　　　　　　　　　　　　　2012001061

British Library Cataloguing-in-Publication Data
A catalogue record for this book is available from the British Library.

Printed in Singapore.

To my friends and students in Singapore

✳

Acknowledgements

❋

Iam a firm believer that thinking is essentially a social process. What I commit to paper is distillation of insights gained from dialogues with oneself and with numerous other people, individually and in groups. I hereby acknowledge the contributions of close friends in Princeton to my current theoretical and practical positions. I mention in particular my friends in Princeton, New Jersey — Arthur Eschenlauer, and Suresh Chugh, former participants of my seminars in JP Morgan, and current business and community leaders.

I am grateful to Dr. Jim Beshai who drew my attention to the work of the great Erwin Straus, where I found scientific support of my naïve insights concerning the upright posture as a distinctive feature of the human person.

I acknowledge the hidden contributions of former students in Rutgers University and thousands of participants of three decades of seminars which I conducted in the United States, Europe, Australia, and South East Asia, particularly in Singapore.

There are a number of associates I must single out, who engaged me in dialogues thus keeping the spark alive in my mind. I must thank Robert Marino for volunteering to read the entire manuscript word for word providing invaluable comments about ambiguity here and there. I thank him in particular for his dedicated spotting of punctuation and typographical errors that had escaped me.

I am especially fortunate to have Susan Miller design and layout the text, figures and tables, along with the cover design of the book itself.

Then there are a number of people whose contributions are more indirect, and yet of great importance. There is Jessie Chan who supported me for more than a decade in running surveys in several organizations in Singapore. Much of the material in the sections on managerial tasks derives from the surveys she managed with me. Jeya Ayadurai provided, and chaired, several forums where I had the opportunity to test my views.

I must thank Siew Lee Loke, my long-time supporter in running my seminars in Singapore. Her hidden contributions do not escape my notice. I am also grateful to the staff of the Temasek Leadership Center under the leadership of Tracy Lee for facilitating my work in Singapore.

Finally, special gratitude is due to World Scientific Publishing, and to my editor, Kim Tan. As always, her expertise in editing and managing the production of this book has been invaluable.

Contents

✳

✳

INTRODUCTION

✳

CHAPTER TWO

The Human Person 43

＊

CHAPTER THREE

＊

CHAPTER FOUR

✳

CHAPTER FIVE

Social Structures   119

✻

CHAPTER SIX

✻

✻

WORK, MANAGEMENT, AND THE BUSINESS OF LIVING

INTRODUCTION

HISTORY OF IDEAS

YOU CANNOT NOT MANAGE

I find it hard to start this introduction without referring to my life experience. Nothing in this book has been planned in advance. I did not set out guided by an outline nor by a plan of reading and researching. Rather, everything came in the course of living. In essence, this book is a record of an epoch in my professional career. It is impossible to identify a specific point in time where the book came into existence. *How could I?* After all, life is an incessant flow of time over which we have no control. It is therefore left to me to choose when my account could begin. I see myself as a clinical psychologist at the Neuro-Psychiatric Institute in Princeton, the university town in the State of New Jersey. The institute was a state mental health organization, not part of Princeton University. My job at the Institute involved three distinct but related responsibilities:

a.   provide diagnostic reports on mental patients to psychiatrists. My reports were based on interviews I conduct and psychological tests I administer;

b.   conduct psychotherapy sessions for various types of patients; and

c.   research.

I think I was happy doing what I was required to do. I learnt later from management literature that my happiness was called *work motivation,* or more specifically, *job satisfaction.* At the same time I was serving as Adjunct Professor in the psychology department of Rutgers University where I taught psychology courses. Teaching at Rutgers added a feature of variety to my professional activities. Furthermore, it provided continuity of my primary academic career.

One day I received a directive from management to attend a course in management provided by the State of New Jersey. I went to my boss to inform him that I would not attend. I explained why I intend to decline the invitation, "I am not a manager. I am a psychologist." My boss pointed out that attendance is mandatory for any state official who assumes supervisory responsibilities irrespective of the official's specialized expertise. I thought then that management was a profession in its own right, a highly developed specialty confined to people in charge of business or government institutions. That was the first time I realized that while being primarily a psychologist I was also a *supervisor.*

Finally, I attended the course. I spent three days feeling bored throughout. I was bored simply because much of what was said touched upon what I was actually doing, though without much thinking. For example, there was reference to *leadership* which I was actually exercising over a number of staff psychologists. Leadership could also extend to my role as a professor in relation to students. There was reference to *appraisal* of employees, exactly what I have been doing with my staff at the institute, or with my students at the university. There was reference to budgeting, purchasing supplies, hiring and disciplining, attending and chairing committees, all of which constituted essential aspects of my job. It seems odd in retrospect that prior to attending the course none of these managerial tasks had entered my mind. I must have been performing them mechanically without much awareness. The most significant outcome of attending the course was the realization that I have been a manager all along. What a revelation!

I was reminded of a character in the French play, *Le Bourgeois Gentilhomme,* one of the masterpieces of Molière. In this play, Molière portrays the character of Monsieur Jourdain, a ridiculous snob aspiring to become a cultured citizen *of quality* like the nobility of his time. Monsieur Jourdain hired a teacher to help him achieve such social status. In one of the lessons, the teacher taught him that language could be either prose or verse. "What is prose?" asked Monsieur Jourdain. "Prose is what you are speaking right now," replied the teacher. Monsieur Jourdain was thrilled to discover that he had been able to speak prose even before he received any teaching. Unable to contain his excitement, Jourdain rushed to his wife boasting, "You ignorant woman, I am able to speak prose!" Fortunately, I kept to myself the discovery that I have been a manager; thus, I escaped the ridicule that Jourdain had received from his wife.

The specialized title of psychologist tended to eclipse the managerial tasks all of which were necessary to fulfill my role as a psychologist. Henceforth, I had to confront these tasks right on. It is true that what I learnt had a negligible effect on my subsequent performance as a psychologist. However, as such tasks come to one's attention, one tends to be deliberate in effecting them.

FIRST ENCOUNTER WITH MANAGERS

Soon after this brief course, I was invited to participate in a management development program to be offered by Rutgers University for AT&T managers. The program was named *Rutgers Advancement Management Development Program* or RAMP. It was a new venture championed jointly by the Extension Division of the university and the Graduate School of

Business Administration. AT&T was then a monopoly, a colossal corporation. In fact it was the second largest employer in the USA, second only to the federal government. Initially, I thought, it would be preposterous to teach these powerful and experienced managers what they have been doing for years. The professor in charge of RAMP was an expert in Industrial Psychology. Besides, he was familiar with my work both at my institute and in his department of psychology. Somehow, he was confident that my *experience* as psychologist was relevant. To temper my anxiety, he gave me a few management textbooks.

After a glance at the content of one of the books, I realized that even absorbing the content of the book would not qualify me to *teach* such a group of experienced managers. After all, teaching requires more than conveying information that has been stored in the teacher's memory. It is the experience that matters — being aware of the implications of what you teach and having engaged in numerous dialogues with various people and with yourself about the subject matter.

I thought of my first encounter with management as a profession in the New Jersey seminar. An idea sprang in my mind — just as I had realized earlier that my role as psychologist had a managerial component, there was bound to be a psychological dimension to the role of a manager. Maybe I could show the AT&T managers how psychological awareness would do justice to their experience, thus enhancing their leadership role. I felt confident about this solution to my dilemma. Finally, I went to my colleague to return his books and to convey my acceptance of the assignment. I felt that I had a decent entry to a new situation: rather than wandering in the dark alleys of business, heretofore a world alien to me, I would instead bring the audience into the world I was familiar with. *But how would I do that?*

To answer this question I have to take the reader back to what I have done in my field in the Neuro-Psychiatric Institute. My main contribution was drawing attention to the primacy of changes of perception in mental disorder, particularly in schizophrenia. I mean perception of objects, appearance of people, time and space. I pointed out that such are the early symptoms in the evolvement of mental illness. And it is such changes that easily escape the attention of psychiatry. Usually patients seek psychiatric help after the breakout of major symptoms such as hallucinations, delusions, and flagrantly bizarre behavior.

My research further argues that thinking disorders (reasoning) and bizarre behavior can be satisfactorily explained in terms of the changes that occurred in the patient's perception of the world. I could conclude that the tragedy of mental illness, particularly schizophrenia, lies in dramatic change and stability of the patient's *world view*. Furthermore changes in the world view bring about fluctuations of mood and serious disruption in interpersonal relationship. In other words, the patient's state resembles that of an exile.

I went back to my lecture notes of the early sixties and found the following paragraph:

> It is impossible to understand people without exploring their *experiential* worlds. Instead of looking *into* people searching for motives, complexes, etc., we [must] try to place ourselves in their place and view the world from their viewpoint. Thus, the psychologist's role becomes similar to that of an anthropologist who tries to map out the world of a culture that is alien to him. Typically, the anthropologist must rely on a *native* as a guide or interpreter. Similarly, the psychologist has no alternative but to establish an authentic dialogue with the individual [patient]. Only through the [other] individual can we explore his world. We [psychologists] have the conceptual framework which determines what we look for, how to bring order to the apparent chaos and how to make sense of what appears to be strange, bizarre, or senseless.

Psychologist as anthropologist! A flash of insight so compelling that it determined my subsequent approach as a psychologist. A psychologist, I thought, does not impose his world view on any patient. Rather, the psychologist should establish a dialogue with the patient, a dialogue geared towards the discovery of the patient's world. At the same time, the psychologist explains to the patient the influence of perception on thinking, feelings, and interpersonal relations. I called the dialogue a process of *shared perception*. A simple and self evident truth, *shared perception* is the key to being together.

Naturally the AT&T managers I was about to encounter were healthy and well-functioning individuals. The way they perceive the world is significantly different from that of the patients I dealt with. Still, healthy individuals develop different world views but these views are essentially constant. Furthermore healthy individuals are able, more or less, to make sense out of the different views of one another. They are also able to correct others' misperception and build relationships based on a modicum of *shared perception*. I decided then that shared perception would afford me a decent entry into my encounter with the audience at RAMP. So much of my knowledge could flow from this core concept that I would then feel at home with the audience.

I still vividly recall my first encounter. While being introduced, I thought that I would start by explaining my position and where I came from. I prefaced my speech by an admission, "I know nothing about management, but I think I know something about people. I come to you from a mental hospital dealing with mental patients." I told them that one lesson I learnt was "You cannot know what goes on in the mind and heart of the other person unless that person lets you in." It hit me that what I learnt about the patient applies more strongly in interaction with the healthy individuals you meet at work and elsewhere. However, healthy individuals have the means to *conceal* their thoughts and feelings, whereas patients reveal them in symptoms which they may or may not be aware of. I borrowed an analogy from late Humphry Osmond, a British psychiatrist I worked with at the time. Most of what goes on in the life of the other individual, notes Osmond, is invisible to us. It is as if the concrete person we see and deal with inhabits an *invisible bubble*. In your encounter with any person, what you actually witness is a single individual.

But in reality that individual is the center of a universe inaccessible to your senses.

Therefore, it would be prudent to bear in mind that an individual you encounter is but a pivot of a complex network of relationships as real as what you actually see, a historical entity with past and future, actualities and possibilities. I remember quoting Karl Jaspers, "The truth begins when two people meet." Understanding requires a map, mapping the world in which you live and the world in which the other person lives. The parameters of the map are identical but the content is different. I went on elaborating the parameters of a world view — the physical world which includes objects, nature, animals and one's own body in as much as the body is a physical entity occupying space along with other physical objects. In addition, there are self image and the image we form of other people around us. In a nutshell this was the core of my message to AT&T managers. Fortunately, the ideas I presented gave rise to rich exchange and animated discussion throughout the two days allocated to me.

At the conclusion of my second day, I received a standing ovation from seminar participants. *What a surprise!* I start out with the admission of my ignorance of management, yet I end by getting a dramatic show of approval from such a seasoned group of managers. Naturally I welcomed the ovation as being a generous reward. But the *meaning* of the ovation deserves a moment of reflection. What I offered must have satisfied a basic need beyond what the mangers had expected to get from a management seminar. I had talked about what is essentially human, not just professional or work-related. The managers gained insights that clarified issues in their life. And clarity of mind is always associated with a euphoric reaction. And it is the euphoric reaction, I thought, which prompted the standing ovation. Subsequently, the managers wrote in the required feedback, "Keep El-Meligi on the job." So I continued to participate in the program for about three years. It so happened that the Graduate School of Business was co-sponsor of the program. Apparently reports about my performance were sent regularly to the school of business. While in the institute one day, I received an offer of professorship.

PSYCHOLOGIST IN BUSINESS SCHOOL!

What could I say? The offer was very gratifying as recognition of a job well-done. More importantly, I welcomed the offer for two reasons: first, it allowed me to return to academia, which I had always considered home. Secondly, it promised a fresh and exciting venture where I would enjoy the freedom to experiment. I leap forward now to the next scene: being interviewed by the dean of the Graduate School of Business in a spacious but unassuming office. On the wall behind the dean, I noted a painting of a player of American football. The painting was modern art with subtle colors and inspiring vigor and sweetness at the same time. The painting told something about the character of the dean.

The painting on the wall distracted me for a while, but in my eagerness to dispel any belief that I claim expertise in management, I wanted to make sure that the offer was not based on an erroneous belief in my competence in management. I hastened to tell the dean, "I never studied management, and I never worked in a business school." "That is why we want you," replied the dean instantly and emphatically. Then, I asked the dean, "What do I teach?" "Pick up any subject from the curriculum or design your own," replied the dean. With these words, the clinical psychologist was ordained a Professor of Management in a School of Business Administration. Such anomaly could not happen except in America at least to my knowledge. Incidentally, 'Business Administration' was soon dropped from the school name. It became *Graduate School of Management*. I welcomed the change. It was a good omen as far as I was concerned, though the change had nothing to do with me. Subsequent to the meeting with the dean, I pondered, *how could my lack of experience in management justify hiring me as full professor?* I thought that the dean must have made up his mind long before we met. He must have based his decision on reports he had received about my performance in RAMP. I then dropped the subject until further notice.

Soon afterwards, a journalist appeared in the school to interview that *strange specimen* recently imported to a school of business! The journalist's opening question was: "What is a clinical psychologist doing in a business school?" I quipped, "humanizing business." I laughed at my own half-serious reply, but the journalist did not. She went on recording what I have just said. Pondering my reply later on, it seemed to make a great deal of sense. *Yes, indeed, that is what I should be doing, humanizing management.* My words reverberated in my mind. I did not imply that management was inhumane. Rather, I thought, it has grown into a specialized profession practiced by experts. That specialty seemed too remote from daily life of ordinary people at home or in the street. Maybe it is about time to liberate management from the confines of the board room of corporations.

Actually I had started my project in RAMP without conscious intention. In retrospect, what I did in RAMP seemed to be my first step in humanizing management. I thought that the first step toward this goal would be to teach MBA students that a professional manager should pay heed to common sense foundations of his/her science. After all, science as we know it today had its rudiments in the most primitive of human minds. Pre-scientific thinking is not always unscientific. Even the most sophisticated scientist in modern times inevitably resorts to common sense and intuition when faced with fresh challenging problems.

MEMBERSHIP BEGINS

Becoming a member is a unique and complex experience. The official appointment occurs on a legal document, but ushers in the process of inclusion into a new environment. I would like to give a brief account of the moment when I felt included as a member of the school. The opportunity was the annual faculty meeting marking the beginning of a new school term. The agenda of the meeting included, among other topics, electing members for the Appointment and Promotion Committee — the most powerful committee in the school. In his capacity as Chairman of the meeting, the dean asked for nominations. Few professors nominated themselves or others. The dean looked at me and asked directly, "Moneim, won't you like to include your name?" Without any hesitation, I said, NO. After the meeting the chairman of my department took me on the side and said, "Why did you turn down the dean's request?" "Turn down?" I replied, "He was just asking me. I did not want to compete for a post I did not particularly want." The chairman said emphatically, "Moneim, the dean was not asking you, he was telling you." That was something I never thought of. I suddenly realized that a university, like any other institution is bound to be a political environment — asking is telling and you are supposed to know when asking means telling.

I thought that the issue ended there, but a few days thereafter, while inspecting the mail delivered at home, I found an official letter from the dean's office. The letter was very brief and to the point. It reads:

> "I would very much like to have you serve as the Dean's appointment to the School's Appointments and Promotions Committee for the 1975–1976 academic year. This is a very important assignment since you [will] contribute importantly to helping me shape the nature of the School and its faculty. I would appreciate a prompt response since I would like to announce it at the next faculty meeting."

I noted that the dean ended the letter by a firm demand, "I would appreciate a prompt response since I would like to announce it at the next faculty meeting." I thought that this time the dean is not only 'telling', but ordering. This man was one of the greatest leaders I came across in my career. His competence shows clearly in the letter despite its brevity. First, he asserted his legitimate right to have me as *the dean's appointment.* Second, he demanded prompt response. Obviously he has the *will to lead* and the *intention* to get what he wanted. Third, he pointed out the rationale for his decision, "to contribute importantly to helping me shape the nature of the School and its faculty." Reading the dean's letter represented a significant experience of becoming a full member of my new environment. My membership has been realized by a *role* in the community beyond my comfort zone within the confines of the classroom. I must add that my work in the Committee added depth to my understanding of how an institution renews itself through the mechanisms of recruitment and promotion.

Reminiscing upon my first meeting with the dean, I understood one reason why he hired me despite my admission of ignorance of management. When the dean appointed me, he was not arbitrary as I had suspected then. He was clear in his mind about the connection between recruitment of a new staff member and his strategy for the school as a whole. A year later I found out one more reason — AT&T was planning to celebrate the 50th anniversary of the Hawthorne experiment. The dean received a request from the organizing committee to appoint a professor to represent the school in the 50th anniversary of the historical experiment in the Hawthorne Works in Michigan. That famous experiment had ushered in the human relations movement in the psychology of work motivation. Being the only psychologist in the school, I was appointed by the dean to represent the school.

Returning to the subject of what courses to teach, I went through the school curriculum and stopped at one course title, *Problems in Personnel Administration*. Fortunately, the course description appeared loose enough to allow me to redefine it in my own way. The word 'personnel' was immediately translated in my mind to *persons* as individuals or as groups. I stopped at the word *Administration*. I thought, "Is it correct to say that we *administer personnel* or administer systems, methods, rules, and the like?" I was not sure, so I went to Random House dictionary where the term *administration* is given eight definitions as follows:

1. The *management* and direction of a government, business, institution, or the like.

2. The *function* of a political state in exercising its governmental duties.

3. The *duty* or duties of an administrator.

4. A *body* of administrators or executive officials.

5. The *officials* of the executive branch of a government.

6. The *period* during which an administrator or body of administrators serves: the Jefferson administration.

7. Law: the *management* of a decedent's estate by an administrator or executor, or of a trust estate by a trustee.

8. The *act* or *process* of administering. [my emphasis]

I noted that 7 out of the 8 definitions are nouns denoting concrete entities — formal systems or bureaucratic organizations. It was the last item in the list which appealed to me for two reasons: First, while it adds nothing to the word itself — administration means to administer. So I am free after all to define it as I please. Second, it denotes a continuous *action*, '*the act or process of administering*'. That may appear tautological but it is not. To manage, to administer, or to lead, is to act on the world — a significant insight, discovery of the obvious. "Think in verbs not in nouns, translate any noun into a verb, only then will you be on the right track," a statement I reiterate in my classes. And yet, something is still missing in the dictionary definition — *administering what?*

I started experimenting with the model which I had outlined in RAMP for AT&T managers. Fortunately, the situation in a university appeared to be more favorable. In RAMP I had only two days — a very confining time space. I felt then like a person who is given a ping pong table on which to play soccer. In the university I had a whole semester to teach more or less the same topic. What a luxury! I decided to include psychological tests in the course with the aim to help MBA students know more about their values, their cognitive styles and their *world view*. This, I thought, would prepare the students to join organizations in the future, as would a smattering of group dynamics and organizations as social systems. One further step in humanizing management, "Management is more than bossing around a bunch of subordinates" became a sort of slogan that I consistently stressed in my classes.

I was fortunate that the move to a business school allowed me to preserve my professional identity as psychologist. This does not imply any value judgment about being a psychologist. I simply imply that I feel more at home and more competent as a psychologist than as something else. However, my approach to psychology is humanistic in nature. Thus my move from a psychiatric institution to a university guaranteed an element of continuity. The conceptual framework I followed in RAMP remained essentially the same. My previous experience must contribute to my new role. But what does that mean? Being in the classroom or in the laboratory I am still a human person rejoicing in the sense of continuity in my life project. *Life project?* I borrowed that expression from existentialist literature. I think it is a fitting alternative to the term *career* — more intimate. Besides it positions work life within the wider context of *living*.

I enjoyed very much being in a university environment for the freedom it afforded. Nowhere could I be freer than in a classroom — I secure a forum for myself with the full autonomy to express my thoughts and feelings, and to a willing audience. I must confess that I tended to exploit this autonomy though for educational or moral purpose. An incident is worth mentioning here. Early one morning, students appeared too passive to give me a hint that they were taking in what I was striving to convey. I felt that my enthusiasm was wasted. Students were just leaning idly on the desks and passively recording whatever words I uttered. I soon came to the realization that my preferred style of dialogue degenerated to sheer dictation. I tried my best to get the students' attention to no avail. With a mixture of shame and anger, I stopped, looked at the class, and protested, "You are not listening and you seem tired, please go home." I collected my papers, looked at the students and repeated loudly enough that they could hear me in their state of semi-slumber, "I am getting bored, go home." I rushed out and headed towards my office thinking, *It is unfair that an audience leaves me alone for three hours. Boredom hurts.* However, I subsequently decided to use this event as an occasion to drive home a lesson during the next class meeting. I prepared a mini lecture on motivation. I stressed the essence of motivation as a two-way process. I told the class, "Students bear as much responsibility to motivate a teacher as the teacher bears to motivate students, reciprocity is mandatory." I added, "Teaching is not just talking. Rather, it is learning. We are here together engaged in a learning enterprise." The reader might apply the same logic to leadership.

Despite my love of academic environment both as a teacher and researcher, I had an aversion to the final examination practice which I experienced as an unnecessary crisis. It was always a period of stress both for the teacher and the students. Often students in the US exercise the right to question the teacher's grading of them. To correct for this problem, I resorted to two procedures: prior to the final exam, I ask students first individually to assess their learning experience and their performance during the term. Secondly, I ask the students to meet as a group to assess the collective performance of the class. This alleviated somewhat the inevitable tension felt by both the students and myself. But still some students, the competitive ones, continued to argue for higher grades. On the positive side, I found out that some students tended to underestimate rather than overestimate their performance.

The course was elective. A large number of students registered for the course, sometimes as many as 50 when usually other classes rarely exceeded 20 students. The popularity of the course turned out to be a curse. Instead of reading about 20 term papers or final exam booklets, I had to toil with 50 or more. The success placed a heavy burden on me. Subsequently, I prevailed on the school to divide the students registering for my course into several sections. Thus, I would be exempted from teaching other courses.

At the end of the term the commencement exercises included the announcement of the *Teacher of the Year* award. I was given this award. That was a pleasant surprise. On the other hand, I was very embarrassed vis-à-vis my colleagues. I worried that being singled out in my first year in the school might not help much my becoming a welcome member in a new environment. However there was nothing I could do about it. It turned out that my embarrassment was due to my own neurotic sensitivity! Collegiality was soon demonstrated in different situations by my colleagues. What is important here is not the award but what the award meant, namely, clear confirmation of my approach. The essence of my approach was to expand management beyond the work place and getting it out of the board room. No more timidity, no hesitance.

ADVISORY ROLE

Shortly after I started teaching a consultancy role was initiated. School policy encouraged professors to engage in outside consulting activities. The school had several reasons for this policy. First, it fosters the image of the school both university-wide and in the business environment. Secondly, professors' teaching is enhanced by practical experience in business firms. The benefit would ultimately filter down to students. Third, contact with business firms was thought to enhance employability of our graduates.

This is not the proper context to provide a full inventory of my consulting experience. I will mention a few that had a strong impact on my experience which, together with later work, contributed immensely to the content and spirit of this book.

Insurance Company: Training Dilemma

A senior executive came to the school to consult with the dean. Apparently, he had approached several business schools to submit proposals for a training program for his senior managers. None of the proposals was approved by management of the firm. The executive confided to the dean that the proposals were turned down not for specific reasons, but because "we really were not clear about what we needed." Finally, he made an interesting suggestion to the dean, "Could you ask one of your professors to visit us and attend certain executive meetings. As an independent observer, the professor may figure out what we really need." I was assigned this task, an awesome undertaking. I cannot go into the details of my meetings, but suffice it to say that the visits enabled me to extract the central topics to deal with and determine the timeframe of the course. The content of the course was based on my direct observation during the meetings I attended and informal conversations with individual executives on different occasions. I came out with a number of insights. I single out below some of these insights.

During the meetings I attended I noted the rich volume of communication, the vigorous exchange of views, mostly evaluative or prescriptive. However, it was difficult for me to arrive at a synthesis of, or clear outcome. Often, I could not tell at the end of a meeting whether consensus was reached. Executives would discuss several issues but no final synthesis would be ventured by any one. I also noted that speakers in the meetings were very eloquent but rarely did they challenge each other. In my conversation with some executives, I sensed that leadership was conceived as effective salesmanship. Dominance and assertiveness constituted the essence of both. Finally, practicality as a value reigned supreme. I made a mental note that the first seminar would focus on assumptions held by managers about leadership. I would promote *conceptualization* to balance out the thrust towards practicality, and argue against dangers of both dominance and efficiency. I would also highlight indications of rigidity and conformity. Clearly, I thought, a system of values which the executives share underlies the aforementioned phenomena. Therefore, reference to organizational culture would be useful.

An anecdote is worth mentioning in this connection. I mention it because the confrontation with a client is an opportunity not only to know something about the client, but more importantly about myself as an academic. I usually submit to the client a brief outline of the central themes of the course followed by a statement of the objectives and desired outcome. Then I had to go through the *ordeal* of deciding the sequence of different topics and delivery time for each. The content of the seminar was approved but there was a snag regarding the timing of different sections. Habitually, I shy away from committing myself in advance to strict timing. I usually indicate time in general designations. For example, 'early morning session', 'late morning session', 'after lunch session', and 'late afternoon', I naively thought this was detailed enough to satisfy any reasonable person. I was wrong. The coordinator appeared shocked by this *looseness.* He demanded more precision in terms of hours. He asked that even time allocated for coffee breaks should be specified. I did what the coordinator wanted. He was pleased with the final version of the outline. Unfortunately, upon further scrutiny of the outline, he discovered 15 minutes unaccounted for. I filled the gap as he wanted. However, I knew that ultimately when time comes for the actual presentation, I would not be bound by any prior script.

I must add, in this connection, that an academic may be inclined to interpret a coordinator's insistence on precise timing as undue *perfectionism* or even as *obsessive compulsive tendency*. But when you know that this gentleman was an expert accountant who was also well-versed in mathematical prediction systems, you would respect his concerns. Meanwhile, his insistence acted as a check on my habitual open-endedness. My ability to talk extemporaneously fits my spontaneity and has its advantages but may also entail serious hazards. Anyhow, the proposal was finally approved and I ran the first seminar as I pleased but with an eye on the clock. Ultimately, managers were pleased despite my violation of the agreed upon strict timing. The managers' satisfaction with the outcome underscores American pragmatism — the end result is what matters most.

It is time to move on to another consulting experience which brought me in touch with an environment dramatically different from the environment of a financial institution.

Strike at a Nuclear Energy Plant

This is the case of a utilities company moving from fossil to nuclear technology. My assignment consisted of two roles, one as a clinical psychologist and the other as management consultant — two quite different roles but related in this case. Regarding the former, federal law required that all applicants to jobs in the nuclear station be screened for mental health. The screening included two procedures, diagnostic interview to be conducted by a psychiatrist and psychological testing to be administered and interpreted by a psychologist. The same procedure was to be repeated on a yearly basis with those who work in the nuclear facility. I was called upon to undertake the psychological assessment. In the preliminary meeting with the coordinator I was informed that the psychological test has already been selected and that management got the approval of the union for the whole assessment procedure. I pointed out that while I approve of the designated psychological test, I felt that one single test would be inadequate. I requested adding one more test to serve the purpose of cross-validation of the results of both tests. I was told that adding one other test to the one already approved would violate the agreement with the union. However, I could use whatever tests I wish to add as an extension of the interview, but not as an additional psychological test. This was acceptable to me.

It was a colossal task which I completed with great satisfaction, since that was exactly what I was doing previously in my career but with different types of people, namely psychiatric patients. In a nuclear facility, the risk was much more serious and requires utmost rigor. I found out that many applicants had prior experience as service men in nuclear submarines. Hence, I learnt a lot about life in this most unusual environment under water. That heightened my sensitivity to the role of environmental context of work.

The other part of my assignment was straight management consulting. It came about as a result of the unexpected strike initiated by the union. The unexpected strike drove management to explore morale. I find myself one day in a nuclear energy plant amid this turmoil. Going into the plant and getting out, I had to submit to a test measuring the amount of nuclear energy that may have seeped into my body, quite anxiety-arousing, but I can assert that I was safe since I survived into my current octogenarian years.

This was by far the gravest assignment in my entire consulting experience. I felt the weight of my responsibility not for the company, not for my reputation, not for the image of the school, but for the world at large. The gravity I felt was not purely subjective. The date is important; it was summer 1982. It was then that a disaster has been averted in the

Three Mile Island accident of 1979 in Pennsylvania. I was not just a scientist, or a university professor, but essentially a world citizen. That forced me to rise in my analysis beyond scientific rigor. My task was fact-finding through interviews of a number of managers at different levels in the authority hierarchy, as well as workers.

I submitted my report. Despite the fact that management was pressing hard for early submission of the report, I heard nothing subsequently. I am not at liberty to share the content of the report since it does not belong to me once it was submitted to the client. But I can share one significant lesson which was best expressed by one of the young managers I had interviewed. He said casually, "You cannot run an atomic energy plant with a fossil mentality." This is a simple common sense statement which nobody can dispute. I would add that revolutionary change of technology requires parallel revolution at a cognitive level.

Profound Concerns About Consulting

My work with the nuclear energy plant got me thinking about the fate of a report a consultant submits to the management of an institution. The report should not be considered the end-product of a consultancy. Rather it should be taken as an input to initiate a dialogue between the consultant and the management of the institution. The aim of the dialogue should be: first, to assess the objectivity of the findings; second, to identify the insights management might have gained from its content and the subsequent dialogue about it. Third, to find out if there were still a need for further enquiry about fresh issues that the report might have raised. Fourth, to explore the practical implications management derive from the exercise in its entirety. After all, management must remain in the driver's seat.

I would like now to move on to a completely different environment, in this case a reputable financial institution. The name is JP Morgan.

FROM ACADEMIA TO WALL STREET

My involvement with JP Morgan (Morgan Guaranty Trust Company as it was called then), happened by accident. A manager had been recently hired to develop management training programs in the bank. He heard about me from a former colleague of his who had attended my RAMP seminars. One day I received a telephone call from him. He invited me to assist him in running an ongoing seminar and plan further training projects. Since I had never heard of JP Morgan prior to the manager's call, I thought that the bank must be a small company. However, I decided to oblige him. I was encouraged by the confirmation I got from both AT&T managers, and later by graduate students in Rutgers Graduate School of Business. By then, the name had been changed to *Graduate School of Management*. Apparently the new title would lend more prestige to the school, an emerging trend in the country. Obviously, words do not differ only in meaning. They also differ in the status we ascribe to them.

Finally, I went to Wall Street for the first time since my arrival in America. Had it not been for this opportunity, I would have never set foot in the financial center of the world. As soon as I got to what is called Wall Street, I had two surprises: First, there was no wall. Second, Morgan occupied 23 Wall Street, a very impressive building. The inside was even more impressive — exquisite taste in furniture, not very businesslike as I had thought a business environment must look like. Things are elegant without exuberance. Decency is the word to describe everything. For example, signs on the doors are small, and more so on bathrooms.

My first program was already in place. It was a 3-day workshop called *Supervisory Development Program (SD III)*. My first assignment in JP Morgan was to take up the last two days of the workshop with the provision of restructuring it in any way I saw fit. A side observation: the title of *supervisor* was considered by many corporations to be of lower status than *manager*. I noticed also the presence of a third title, namely *executive*, denoting the highest level of managers. Since *Supervisory III* was the name of the program, I thought that there must have been versions I & II, for still lower level supervisors. I wondered at the depth of the vertical hierarchy of authority in the bank.

I fit in very quickly in the program but recommended a change — moving the program out of the bank, and changing it into a residential workshop. I chose as venue a conference center in Princeton. One of the earliest features I detected in JP Morgan was welcoming innovation, at least for me. The move had dramatic effect both on motivational level of participants and on my own performance. The evening sessions gave more time for interaction among participants and ample opportunity for extra-curricular activities.

After teaching for nearly one year, I happened to address participants in the workshop as 'bankers', and before I could complete my statement, several voices interrupted, "We are not bankers." Baffled, I asked, "What are you then in a bank if not bankers?"… "We are managers of bank operations," replied several participants. For more than a whole year I took it for granted that my audience were all bankers. I realized suddenly to my surprise that people working in the bank are not necessarily doing banking business. How could that be? Bankers deal with clients, they generate income. Bank operations are often called something else, *back-office personnel* — a reminder of administrators versus academicians in a university, or medical staff versus administrators in a hospital, etc. *Do not take labels seriously* — that was a lesson I learnt about diversity of functions even in the most specialized institutions such as banks. Other than bankers and traders who generate profits directly, there were what might be called *ancillary services* such as bank operations, accountants, auditors, financial analysts, human resource specialists, corporate communication, and more. I realized that without the *ancillary personnel*, bankers could not generate profit. Nonetheless, back-office personnel were seen by profit centers to be peripheral to business. Consequently, they earned less than the bankers and their jobs were considered less prestigious. I concluded that a modern corporation does not escape the contradictions existing in society at large — class differences pervade corporations. After all, an organization is necessarily a social entity, irrespective of whether its primary function was financial, manufacturing, educational, or otherwise. Note that all those who work for a corporation are members, but with different functions and different levels of social standing or status. The word *membership* continued to intrude into my mind since. Initially, I did not ponder its implications. Surprisingly and fortunately, I discovered its rich implications as I will show in this book. But let us return to Wall Street.

The fact that a large mass of personnel working in a bank are not called bankers created some dissonance in my mind. I wondered why *real* bankers are not represented in a management development program. I went to the director of training seeking explanation. By then, the director of training had become a friend that I could level with. I said to him, "It seems odd that a training program is offered to ancillary service personnel, but not to bankers proper." He explained, "We have in place a specialized training program for bankers, which focuses on credit, economics, and various technicalities of banking." I suggested that we extend training in management to the bankers. He immediately approved. By the way, the director was formerly a Harvard professor and was naturally well disposed towards management development. He then approached the *real* bankers with my suggestion. The bankers' response was "We are not managers, we are bankers." That response sounded familiar, I have been there myself. He suggested that we present the idea to bankers in the European offices, which he did. The idea was welcomed immediately by bankers there. I speculated, *could it be that the farther you were from the headquarters the more open will you be to new ideas? Or that those in the headquarters may see themselves as the elite class of the bank?* Such questions, I thought, deserve exploration.

I set out to design a 6-day residential program. I prepared an outline of the main themes and the methodology including lectures, discussion meetings of small groups, and case studies. I included psychological instruments to be administered to participants in an introductory session. Those instruments focused on management styles, personal values, and major personality characteristics. A word is in order here about the use of psychological instruments in management development. I make a distinction between tests given for assessment leading to making decisions affecting test takers, and tests given in training seminars. In a training seminar, the psychological instruments would serve as exercise in self awareness in preparation for the comprehensive learning experience in the seminar itself. Even without receiving the results the exercise is beneficial in itself.

The design I presented to the director of training was deliberately schematic to allow me the freedom of modification and elaboration in the course of the seminar itself. I never thought that a long term program could be final at any time. The reaction of the participants and their views should be taken into consideration. Training, in my view should not be a single event but a process. Only after encounters with the audience could I settle on a definitive content. And even then, the initial design would still remain open to change.

CHOICE OF A NAME

By that time, I had become very careful about what words to choose as a title for the program. I went over the lexicon referring to the subject and stopped at the following words: supervision, administration, management, leadership. I asked myself what these words have in common. A series of associations came to mind: "putting things in order, coordinating, integrating, disciplining, planning, sequencing, and others." All the words that emerge as free associations denote *intervention* in the course of events, deliberate effort to counteract disorder, randomness, or chaos. Ordinarily, such conditions give rise to confusion and uncertainty at a psychological level. The concept of *entropy* — had captured my attention since my work with mental patients in the sixties. I knew of course that entropy is a central concept in thermodynamics. I knew very little then about thermodynamics but as the word gained momentum, and acceptance, I spent a lot of time learning and consulting with engineers about the implications of the second law of thermodynamics.

Organization Behavior was a common course in business schools and psychology departments. I replaced the word *behavior* by management. That was consistent with my theoretical bias which is inimical to excessive behaviorism, so dominant at the time in psychology quarters. Behaviorism considers inner experiences *mentalistic* ideas unworthy of scientific enquiry. So the term organization management instead of organization behavior speaks for my theoretical persuasion that inner experience deserves as much attention as manifest behavior, if not more. I also intended to stress that the organization as collective entity is a function of ongoing activities of organizing, or counteracting entropy. I deliberately avoided the word leadership as the title of the seminar. This is because of the many reservations I harbored against the popular concept of leadership as an intrapersonal phenomenon. I saw leadership as an organizing social phenomenon that should be dealt with in the context of other organizing processes that sustain any social system.

SEMINAR VERSUS TRAINING

My mind jumped forward — *what after the first seminar?* I believe that there is a vast difference between a single seminar and a *training program*. Training should be a long-term process, not a single event or a series of separate events. Training implies continuity of learning. One shot run of a seminar may benefit managers as individuals, but organization development would not necessarily follow. But to my mind, the issue is training for the sake of organizational *self renewal*. Organizational self renewal may even demand more than training programs. Other mechanisms are also needed. This issue will be dealt with later in the current volume. So my seminar alone would not qualify as a *training program* unless it is complemented by a follow-up. I called my first seminar Organization Management I and the later seminar will be Organization Management II.

Continuity from OM I and OM II should be experienced by participants. For that reason I decided that OM I be taken as condition for admission to OM II. Thus the design of OM I had to be set in the light of OM II. Initially, I had in mind a one-year lapse between OM I and OM II to allow sufficient time for those who completed OM I to mull over, and experiment with what they learn in OM I. Moreover, I was not thinking only of participants but also of their respective institutions. I thought this strategy would in the meantime commit the organization to the program as an ongoing integrated project, rather than as a single event.

The first OM I seminar was held in Lausanne, a charming city not far from Geneva and in one of the remaining palaces in Europe called 'Beau Rivage'. The seminar was very well received and word spread bank-wide about its success. Our friends in New York, despite their initial rebuff of the idea, went to the training director confronting him with a protest, "How come you offer a seminar to our branches in Europe and ignore us here in the headquarters!" Concealing a sense of triumph, the director of training 'apologized' and promised to institute the seminar henceforth in the USA.

I began to run OM I seminar in a fine conference center in Connecticut. Later on I changed the site to a conference center just outside Princeton, New Jersey, where I reside. In the meantime, I continued to run the same seminar in Lausanne for European branches. And later on JP Morgan decided to make the seminar available to branches of the bank in the Far East — first in Hong Kong, later in Manila, twice in Singapore and once in Australia.

UNWANTED INSPIRATIONAL IMPACT

The seminar impact on participants was quite intense. Comments by participants included words like *inspirational, self revelation, mind-opener*. Counter to my intent, the impact of my performance — at least in the case of the more impressionable participants — turned out to be more affective than rational or intellectual. I could not dismiss my own responsibility for this impact. This is because it was consistent with comments from participants in RAMP. I recall a comment from few participants in RAMP to the effect that I was a 'gifted evangelist.' That comment, I dismissed as being just awkward compliment. Be that as it may, I decided in future programs to temper the affective tone of my presentation in favor of the rational and theoretical. But how could I do that?

I revised my methodology in the following manner: first, increase the time for free discussion; second, introduce exercises to be undertaken by small groups outside the main classroom. Thus participants are enabled to assume more active role in the learning process. Meanwhile, I need not inhibit my spontaneous style of communication. That change created an optimal balance of the rational and the affective components of the learning process.

A brief word is due about the continuity from OM I to OM II. I thought that continuity must be experienced by participants. Furthermore, depth must be provided to the same concepts discussed in OM I. Examples are: management style offered in OM I would be expanded in OM II to the discussion of authority and use of power. Leadership as a process which pervades different levels of the organization hierarchy would complement leadership as activities performed by individual leaders. More personality traits would be added to extraversion-introversion dimension presented in OM I. In OM I refer briefly to sources of tension and neuroticism as a personality trait. In OM II more elaborate model of stress management would be presented. I also added sessions on conflict both interpersonal and interdepartmental.

ADVISORY WORK

The seminar generated a lot of advisory work for both Morgan headquarters and its branches around the world. Heads of Morgan branches around the world could invite me for consultations or to conduct brief workshops focusing on specific local issues. I developed a wealth of information about issues that challenge managers around the globe. JP Morgan helped a lot in my own research. For example, I was able to visit several firms in

Japan and conduct interviews with Japanese experts on quality control. At one time, I interviewed the president of the union of autoworkers in the midst of a crisis. I visited Nissan factory and several other TV factories and watched Japanese personnel at work.

I think it would be appropriate to point out that my life philosophy was very different in many ways from participants in my seminars in JP Morgan. Nevertheless, at no time did I feel inhibited to express myself. My views were sometimes challenged. The challenge was reciprocal. Debate was always animated and enlivened by humor and enjoyment of the overall exercise. It was also refreshing to note that most of the people who attended my seminar were internationally minded and curious about different cultures, having lived overseas during their professional career.

SINGAPORE ADOPTS THE SEMINAR

An unexpected opportunity presented itself when the seminar was held in Hong Kong for Asian offices of JP Morgan. One of the participants in the Hong Kong seminar was a Singaporean. His name is Lim Ho Kee[1]. During a later visit to Singapore I met with Ho Kee who introduced me to the President of the Development Bank of Singapore (DBS). That ushered in the seminar beyond JP Morgan. I started offering OM I in Singapore in the year 1981. I must acknowledge in this respect Fock Siew Wah[2], another eminent executive whom I had met in JP Morgan. He played a supportive role in expanding the OM project in Singapore. Earlier sessions were offered to senior managers from government-owned companies and later for heads of civil service. The two programs ran parallel to each other for about two years but were subsequently merged. Foreign companies in Singapore were also welcome to enroll participants.

---

[1] At the time I am writing, Lim Ho Kee is Chairman of Singapore Post, a government-owned company currently going through horrendous transformation.
[2] At the time of my writing Fock Siew Wah was Chairman of the Singapore Port Authority. He is responsible for steering the port to become a major global player.

I recall for instance, the Singapore branch of the Union Bank of Switzerland which by that time was headed by Lim Ho Kee who by then had left JP Morgan to pursue his career in the service of Singapore.

Early in 1983, the program crossed the straits to Malaysia. Interestingly this was done in response to a suggestion offered by Lim Ho Kee. Ho Kee is a perfect example of championship, a rare type of leader who adopts a cause and takes pains to realize it. Ho Kee thought that the program would represent an opportunity for leaders from both countries to share the same conceptual outlook. Furthermore Ho Kee and I believed that shared perception would somehow enhance communication and interaction between the two countries. Later on, an Indonesian state bank adopted the program. The enthusiasm of early groups of Indonesian participants promised a long-term relationship. The extension of the seminar beyond Singapore represented unscripted shift in the original mission from a national to a regional program.

FAREWELL TO ACADEMIA

I was still full-time Professor at Rutgers and managed to continue my activities in South-East Asia. The school gave me the freedom for full semester to engage in my consulting activities for Singapore. Later on I was granted a leave of absence for two years. However, my involvement became so engrossing that returning to school felt like unwelcome discontinuity to my involvement in South-East Asia. I dare say that I may have outgrown the constriction of my role at the university. Before the end of the second year of the leave of absence, I requested an extension for one more year, which my department rejected. In a matter of seconds, I picked up the phone and without hesitation I resigned, giving up my tenure. I realized that my membership in the university had grown thin. There was also a pull to Asia where I could see the future of the world being forged.

*

FLASHBACK: REMINISCING

Reminiscing on my first encounter with AT&T managers, I recall telling the managers that I knew nothing about management. My subsequent teaching MBA students and consulting activities provided unassailable evidence that I was utterly wrong. Without formal training in management, I was able to draw on my past experience in various types of institutions, first in Egypt, in universities where I have been student and later a teacher, in hospitals, let alone various other institutions, both governmental and non-governmental. In Egypt I had even participated in the creation of institutions for youth welfare and in reforming other institutions such as prisons. I must add my own experience of my own family, both the nuclear and the extended. That was in Egypt, but shortly after arriving in the USA, I got involved both in academic and non-academic institutions as I mentioned earlier.

The question that comes to mind is, "why did I firmly and sincerely believe that I was ignorant of management the first time I met AT&T managers at RAMP?" I shall try below to provide an explanation of my erroneous admission. It seems that I was *managing* without calling myself a manager. I was *leading* and often *following* without calling myself either leader or follower. I was totally absorbed in delivering, and developing, my expertise. Information about social roles, conflict, power struggle, management or mismanagement, leadership, organizational culture, were daily experiences hitting me from every direction. They were impacting my work, sometimes positively and often negatively. The experiences were random, dispersed, sporadic and disconnected. I was short of a label that would have connected these and brought them under mental control. Like a magic wand, the word 'management' evoked a rich store of knowledge — knowledge that was peripheral moved to occupy central position in my thinking. Events that I had dismissed in the past became relevant if not compelling. As a French writer put it, "Time lends transparency to historical events." The truth of this statement was demonstrated by my professional services to medical research workers in the Neuro-Psychiatric Institute, a turning point in my career. A series of events are worth mentioning.

I mention briefly my unintended involvement in scientific organizations long before I found out that psychologist as I have been, I was also a manager. That was in the 1960s of the last century. I was connected with two state organizations housed together in Princeton: The Neuro-Psychiatric Institute and the NJ Bureau of Research in Neurology and Psychiatry. It was hard to separate these two institutions because scientists in both were interdependent. Scientists at the time were conducting experiments of drug induced biochemical changes in mental patients. They used psychological personality tests to ascertain that the changes they detected in biochemical indices were also shown by changes in psychological indices. Researchers ran into a problem: personality tests which they used did not register any change parallel to the biochemical changes. Researchers were certain about the biochemical change but wondered how changes in the same direction did not show parallel change in the results of the psychological tests they had used.

The head of the research team approached me seeking explanation and possible assistance. As soon as I entered his office, I recall, he pointed at a shelf behind him where he had placed psychological test materials, and said: "Help yourself, these tests are useless." I assured him that the tests he had used were proven to be both reliable and valid in exploring more-or-less stable personality traits in normal individuals. I pointed out that traditionally, psychologists aim in their studies to explore stable personality characteristics. The tests that researchers in the institute were using were not designed to measure changes in normal personality, let alone subtle changes.

Fortunately, I had just completed the design of what came to be known later as the *Experiential World Inventory* or the EWI. My main purpose was to develop an instrument which could be given repeatedly to patients to detect changes in the course of developing disorder or in the course of their treatment. The instrument had proved effective in the detection of disturbances in sensory perception and correlated changes in mood, impulse regulation, and thought control. Those were the changes that are likely to be correlated with physiological changes. Scientists began to use my test in subsequent research. Sure enough, the clinical and physiological changes researchers noted in several trials were corroborated by changes at the psychological level revealed by the EWI. For instance, one line of research by Dr. Pfeiffer and others noted that drop in zinc and rise in copper in the blood serum were correlated with depression as measured by the EWI.[3] This finding has been reported in several publications.

At the same time, the Center for the treatment of alcoholism in the Institute had embarked on an experimental trial of treating alcoholism with LSD. While this regimen appeared promising with almost all alcoholics, it triggered latent psychosis in a few. The need arose for an instrument to screen patients who were susceptible to psychotic breakdown in reaction to LSD. I was called upon to administer my test to all alcoholic patients prior to receiving LSD. I used the EWI in the identification of such patients. Little did I know then that this involvement would change my prior plan to return to Egypt after a stay in America only for a few years. I stayed on to pursue further research.[4]

My work with alcoholics reached the attention of Bill Wilson, the co-founder of Alcoholics Anonymous or AA. He came down to visit me in the Institute. My encounter with Bill Wilson turned out be one of the most inspiring and productive events in my entire career. Besides, it generated several invitations for lectures and consulting activities for institutions engaged in the treatment of alcoholism. A fortuitous event thus expanded my clinical experience beyond schizophrenia. More importantly, it drew my attention to non-profit organizations.

---

[3] Pfeiffer, Carl C. (Ed.) *Neurobiology of the Trace Metals Zinc and Copper.* New York: Academy Press, 1972.

[4] LSD and its therapeutic use. The State of New Jersey had employed Humphrey Osmond, a world authority on LSD and several compounds. Humphry Osmond was my co-author of the EWI.

I would like to take this opportunity to share with the reader significant insights I gained from the story of AA as a global institution.

1. Despair as a Source of Creativity

The concept of AA occurred at the very moment both co-founders realized that they could not recover relying on their own will. I was impressed by the fact that a moment of despair was at the same time a moment of breakthrough in thinking. It gave birth to an enduring global movement in combating alcoholism. Bill Wilson and his cofounder concluded: alcoholism is an illness strictly speaking, not aberration in character even though aberration could be a by-product. It follows that an alcoholic is unable to rid him/herself of addiction relying on traditional therapeutic methods such as medicine, psychiatry, or psychotherapy. Only alcoholics as a community can develop procedures to help themselves. This thought was an intuitive leap, a highly condensed conviction that captured my attention and calling for analysis.

2. The Power of Shared Perception

Alcoholics having been through the same experience are the only people who would understand the nature of their plight. Consequently, they are the only people that can help each other. *Membership* in AA is initiated by the alcoholic's making a public admission, "My name (only the last name) is so and so and I am alcoholic." Members are expected to play a double role of receiving and giving help, leading and following are reciprocal not opposites.

3. The Potency of Spirituality in Revolutionary Change

AA demonstrated the potency of spirituality in revolutionary change, in this case the eradication of addiction. I mean by spirituality here a state of faith that defies reality, not simply as religious conversion or affiliation to a given religious faith.

4. *Championship as Leadership*

I had often met with a rare type of leaders, champions of social causes.[5]
I never thought at the time that my involvement with alcoholics was
indeed relevant to the discipline that was called management. I apologize
for lingering on my subjective experience with AA movement, but
subjectivity sometimes generates facts on the ground. It would be a great
loss if we dismiss the role of intuition in altering bitter realities.

It is time now to have a fresh look on the preceding historical account as a
whole and extract some general lessons that benefit people in managing
their lives, professional or otherwise.

LEARNING IS A TWO-WAY PROCESS

As you teach, you discover gaps in your knowledge. The discovery comes
about in response to questions from the audience, questions that you
were unable to answer, or could only answer in a manner that proved
unsatisfactory to you. You then take it upon yourself to fill in the gaps of
knowledge by further reading, researching, and more thinking. Below I
cite examples of learning received from the audience I was invited to teach.

CAPTURING ELUSIVE INSIGHTS

A seminar participant told me that in the course of my lecturing, novel
ideas spring in his mind as *revelations*. Sometimes, a statement I had
uttered impress him as a maxim. "Unfortunately," he added, "I lose the
emory of such ideas or statements despite my belief at the time that they
would be fixed for ever in my mind." For this reason, the participant

---

[5] Incidentally, the community as a therapeutic environment had been recognized in Africa
long before the founding of AA. Local psychiatrists trained in the West discovered the
futility of mental hospitals for the treatment of mental patients. When they returned to
practice in their countries, they started using the village as the therapeutic environment.

suggested, that I design "some kind of journal in which participants record insights day by day." I designed a *Daily Journal* with guiding instructions related to the central topics I dealt with in class. This became a standard procedure which I kept modifying guided by other participants' comments and by my own insights. Now I introduce this journal during the introductory session of any of my seminars. I stress the fact that precious insights are like dreams, they are most likely to be forgotten. I urge participants to record at the end of the day or during the class sessions what they consider unexpected new learning. Fortunately, students were generous enough to send back to me some of my statements that impressed them as quotes worthy of preserving. They referred to them as *Moneim's throwaways*. In retrospect, I realize that my teaching included actual training in the use of intuition. Since then, I repeat to every audience the statement, "Never dismiss your intuition, but test it." What is the rationale for not dismissing intuition? The answer is that intuitive insights do not come from nowhere. They consist of information stored in the unconscious about events that occurred at sometime in the past. *But why test it?* The answer is that the information may be erroneous.

Two situations come to mind. I usually advise organizations to apply two criteria in the selection of managers who attend OM I. My primary criterion is that a participant must have acquired enough experience managing subordinates. Second, the manager should not be too close to retirement. The rationale for the first criterion is that experienced managers would have encountered enough difficulties and challenges that would enable them to build on their prior experience and confront their own assumptions and habit systems. The rationale for the second criterion is that returning participants would still have enough time to give the benefit of their new learning to the organization to which they belong. I would like to mention two incidents where my advice was overlooked or ignored.

The first incident occurred in Malaysia. Senior government officials in Malaysia were enrolled in OM I seminar, presumably "to upgrade their leadership skills." During the orientation session, I found out to my surprise that most of these officials were close to retirement. In fact, a few of them were already due to retire within months subsequent to their attendance of the seminar. One would not expect such individuals to be concerned with leadership as much as with challenges of retirement. In view of my broad conception of management as a universal human burden, I could easily shift the emphasis from leading a formal organization to managing personal and family resources throughout retirement years. After all, retirement years in my model of personality features as a phase in an *integrated life project*.

My second example comes from a government organization in Singapore. The head of human resources, who had attended both OM I & OM II believed that training programs should serve the purpose of *organization development*. Carried away by his enthusiasm, he decided to extend the benefit of the seminar to lower level employees, new recruits included. In the orientation session I discovered that most young participants were newcomers to their organization. For some, current jobs were their first experience having come out of the university recently. On the positive side, they appeared very motivated to learn. Indeed, they felt flattered to have been granted the same opportunity as their seniors. And yet, here they were "to upgrade, or discover, their leadership potential."

The immediate concern of these young employees was much more banal and more pressing than leadership, namely how to fit into a new environment as active and worthwhile *members*. More specifically, they were faced with the challenge of adapting to supervisors different in roles and expectations from the professors they had left behind. Then there was another change for these graduates to contend with, namely the time span. In the university they knew the beginning and the end of the period required for graduation. Whereas in the business world, time span is indefinite, a career that extends into the unknown future. Consequently, the skills they had acquired in dealing with professors could not be applicable to dealing with their supervisors. More importantly, the institution they had recently joined seemed mysterious by comparison to the university environment. We come, once more, to the challenge of fitting in as *members*. The newcomers to a formal organization must learn how to carve a career in a new, *alien* environment. Some of these young men and women could not care less about leadership. Instead many were hoping to develop careers in research and meanwhile rejoin the university seeking higher degrees. Only a minority entertained the desire to become "leaders of people," to use the expression of one participant.

I was faced with a dilemma — to insist on running the seminar as if the audience were *bona fide* managers would be absurd. I decided to turn the objective away from how to lead other people to how to carve a career in a business organization. Again, the conception of management as a universal process provides the opportunity to talk about the business of living anywhere.

INFLUENCE OF THE ENVIRONMENTAL CONTEXT

My seminars were discontinued twice due to dramatic political upheavals in two countries. The seminars for JP Morgan were discontinued in Manila, subsequent to the fall of President Marcos. Similarly Singapore seminars were discontinued in the aftermath of the revolution that toppled President Suharto. At the time, Singapore seminars were conducted in Batam, an Indonesian island in the vicinity of Singapore. Furthermore, the seminars in Jakarta for Indonesian state banks could not be resumed, despite a promising start. It is significant that dramatic changes at a global level would encroach directly on a management development program. These events brought home to me with full force that even the most local of activities does not escape the intrusion of the most global of happenings.

HOUSEHOLD MANAGEMENT

In the last evening of any of my seminars I conduct one-hour *consulting sessions* for small groups of 6 to 8 participants. Attendance was voluntary and yet most participants register for attendance. The purpose of the sessions was to clarify ambiguities or other difficulties which the participants may have encountered during the class meetings. Furthermore, participants would have the opportunity to explore the practical implications of what they have learnt. The topics for discussion were to be determined by those who participated. One more purpose of the sessions was to help integrate the many themes dealt with in the main sessions.

I soon discovered that many situations in business firms have their counterparts in the family environment. Seminar participants would shift smoothly from identification of management styles to parental styles; use and abuse of power, a central topic in OM II, shed light on the power struggle within the nuclear family or between married couples and their in-laws; use of coercive power, in particular, led to heated controversy in connection with the practice of physical punishment in bringing up children. Furthermore, participants could apply what they learnt about group dynamics to the family as a primary social group. It was interesting to note that seminar vocabulary enabled participants to look at household problems in a more objective manner and with less emotional involvement. To that extent, I would agree with many participants' comments that the seminars had therapeutic effect.

Issues related to household management began to surface with increased frequency in recent years. This came as a result of the increased number of women participants both in Malaysia and Singapore. In Malaysia, the sight of women clad with headscarves would conceal from an outside observer the fact that these women held responsible leadership positions, let alone that they were competing successfully in a world that was until recently exclusive of them. I recall in one OM I seminar in Singapore there was a woman participant with the rank of police commander. She impressed her fellow participants by her intellectual outlook and managerial acumen. Interestingly, she would skip lunch with the rest of participants, rushing home to check on her children, and return on time to participate in the afternoon session.

LANGUAGE BARRIER

My seminars in both Malaysia and Singapore have been facilitated by the fact that participants in both countries were proficient in the English language. That was to be expected since it was the policy in both countries to institute the English language as the primary language in education. In Indonesia the situation was different. Proficiency in English language was weak, at best. I wondered how I could run a 6-day seminar in English which was not even the secondary language in the educational system of Indonesia. To cope with the language barrier, I set up a strategy of three measures. First, I prepared an English-Indonesian lexicon of the key words in the lectures or in the pre-seminar questionnaires.[6] Second, I extended the length of the seminar from six to seven days. The additional day would be devoted to the study of the lexicon. Third, in small group discussions, participants would be free to use the Indonesian language, with the provision of one member who was proficient in English. That member was assigned the task of reporting group deliberations to the meetings of the entire class. I think the three measures helped overcome the language barrier. In fact, the lexicon received positive comments in the final feedback reports submitted by seminar participants.

On the whole, I experienced smooth passage from addressing Westerners to addressing Asians. The population I was dealing with, particularly in Singapore and Malaysia, were somewhat westernized. Furthermore, participants were up-to-date with regard to scientific and technological advances in the West. Many had earned degrees from Western universities, often with distinction. Encouraged by the smooth transition from addressing Western audiences to Asians, I did not look closely enough to detect significant difference that existed between Asian audiences and their Western counterparts. The difference turned out to be more historical or situational than essentially cultural.

---

[6] The Malay language is called Bahasa. It has two slightly different versions in Malaysia and Indonesia. They are Bahasa Melayu and Indonesia Melayu.

*

FLASHBACK: OM SEMINARS

I will try to explain as much as I could gather. I had landed in Singapore the first time in 1980. The country had gained independence 15 years earlier (in 1965). That is a very short time relative to the history of a nation. It took me sometime before I realized that Singapore participants were not just leaders in their respective organizations, but *citizens* engaged in *nation building*. And it did not take long for Singapore graduates of OM seminars to grow into a critical mass in their respective institutions. Several institutions began to look at the OM seminar as *core curriculum* from which more specialized workshops could be derived. In response to demand, I designed a series of workshops, shorter in duration than OM. Such workshops focused on issues of interest to single organizations. The following workshops were requested by different government departments or private corporations: *Management of Change and Continuity; Interpersonal Communication; Self Management; Stress Management,* and others.

Among the organizations that requested one or the other of specialized workshops are the following:

- *Singapore Airlines* (SIA), the best in the world both in terms of profitability, excellence in service, and technological innovation, not to mention exuding Asian grace.

- *Urban Redevelopment Authority* (URA) charged with the mission of designing the island of Singapore as envisioned 30 years into the future. Scarcity of land had to be faced head on.

- *Government Investment Corporation* (GIC), managing the wealth of Singapore.

- *Development Bank of Singapore* (DBS) striving to become a major regional financial institution.

- *Singapore Post*, striving to compete with foreign companies right in

Singapore and thriving to change from the traditional mail service to new businesses in a global environment.

- *Public Utilities Board* (PUB) managing the water resources of the island. Scarcity of water resources has compelled the Singapore authority to make utmost use of technical ingenuity and creative potential of its technical staff. Having satisfied local needs for water, PUB began to offer the fruits of its expertise to countries around the world. Shortage of water has been turned from a strategic vulnerability into a strategic advantage with the environment and water industry earmarked as a key growth sector of the economy.

- *Academy of Law* asked me to run a workshop designed specifically for lawyers engaged in business mediation.

How about the parallel situation in Malaysia? Malaysia had earned independence a few years before Singapore. In Malaysia, I ran workshops for the following:

- *Law Enforcement Institutions*, which brought together prison wardens, police commissioners, physicians, and administrators. Management of prisons expanded my conception of management beyond industrial and commercial firms. Meanwhile, I realized the universality of the challenge of integration that arises as a result of specialization.

- My consulting and teaching activities provided *direct contact with audiences from all levels of education*, from the primary to university levels. Regarding the former, I was invited to visit primary schools in the province of Pahang, Malaysia. In each school, I was required to address teachers and my lectures were instantly translated into Malay language. Lectures were followed by free discussion of the challenges the teachers were facing at the time. I found out, among other problems, that the teachers felt inferior to their counterparts in secondary schools. I countered this phenomenon by pointing out the fact that the primary school teacher occupies a unique position in the educational scheme of the country. It is the primary school teacher who takes over the task of child rearing from the parents. In other words, the primary school teacher manages the child's transition from the intimate atmosphere of family life to the public sphere in the school environment. As such, the primary school teacher plays a significant role in nation building. I added that the transition is often too abrupt and too harsh for children. For this reason, I believe that the role of the primary school teacher should be that of a specialist in child rearing such as a pediatrician in medicine. Until we have such specialist teacher, education authorities must provide schools with sufficient numbers of child psychologists to complement the educational efforts of the teacher, particularly in the case of problem and exceptional children.

- Regarding the *secondary school level*, I conducted workshops for directors of education. I was pleasantly surprised that educational authorities in Malaysia had dealt with the dilemma of the teacher who would prefer to spend his or her entire career in classroom: how to respond to that need without the penalty of missing regular promotions and increased income. I discovered that the Ministry of Education allowed teachers to remain as class teachers without losing the opportunities of regular promotions in rank and compensation. The teacher was given the honorary title of super teacher. I learnt later that Singapore had the same practice.

- More recently (2008) a new organization emerged in Malaysia, the *Academy of Higher Education (Akademi Kepimpinan Pengajian Tinggi) (AKEPT)*. The mission of the academy is to enhance leadership quality in institutions of higher learning in Malaysia. AKEPT adopted OM seminars as integral part of leadership training targeting university Vice Chancellors, Deputy Vice Chancellors, and Deans of private and public universities. OM seminars thus provided me with a glimpse into the entire educational system of Malaysia from the primary to the university level.

All the afore-mentioned experiences compelled me to bear in mind that Singapore and Malaysian participants came to my seminars with a mental set different from that of the Western participants who had attended the same seminars in USA or in Europe. While their Western counterparts were keen to upgrade leadership skills and develop their managerial know-how, the former were in the first place citizens involved in nation building. My realization of this feature must have closely influenced both the content of my presentations and teaching method.

I must add that teaching and consulting in both Singapore and Malaysia had the positive side effect of upgrading my knowledge of societies in South-East Asia. Soon after I started teaching, I became aware that I was learning as much as I was teaching. However, the classroom was not the only source of my learning. A great deal of extra-curricular activities and contacts provided me with invaluable opportunities for continued education.

I have come to the end of the historical account of my intellectual journey in as much as it generated the ideas that make up the current book. I advise the reader to review the previous pages and note all the words which appear in italics. I deliberately marked them in italics to stress the fact that they represent concepts that were triggered by circumstances in my professional life. The reader may consider them *keywords* around which the content and method of the book will revolve. Words like *shared perception, world view, entropy, contextual thinking, psychologist as anthropologist, humanizing management, membership, leader as follower, leader and followers as members, roles as actualized membership, household management, learning as two-way process*, and several others occurred as flashes of insight. Some of these words were already known and I have previously encountered in the course of my studies or readings. But in my case, they were insights extracted from real life experiences. These insights could subsequently be connected together in a logical fashion. Therefore, the reader may take my historical account as a case study demonstrating the intimate connection between history of ideas and the lived experience of scientists, philosophers, or bearers of culture in general. In other words, the themes constituting this book are the end product of the author's decades of experience.

CHAPTER TWO

THE HUMAN PERSON

DON'T THINK, JUST LOOK!

Fifty years as a practicing psychologist and trained philosopher, I start from the realization that we ignore the simple fact that we are human, and that the people we lead are equally human. We forget this because it is self evident, banal, ordinary, and simple, in short *unscientific*. It is as if science were not created to connect us to reality in all its richness and complexity.

One sentence uttered by a genius shook me. He said after years of erudition, "Don't think, just look." This man is Wittgenstein, one of the great philosophers of the twentieth Century. When he was a student at Cambridge, he met two giants of the same century — Bertrand Russell and Alfred North Whitehead. They were already published and eminent in both philosophy and mathematics. They agreed that knowing the young scholar was *the greatest thing that had happened to them*. In fact,

Wittgenstein went to Cambridge forsaking a promising career as an aeronautic engineer and inventor.

Don't be surprised when I tell you that we forget to look, we forget to feel, we forget to be simply human. I spent years reading complicated stuff about leadership until I started to ask people in several countries, "What kind of boss would you like to follow?" The answers I received were far from being technical or 'scientific' — answers such as *polite, courteous, civil, decent, considerate, listens to me*, and similar banal answers. Rarely did I get the sort of sophisticated terms we are familiar with in scientific management such as person-oriented, or bureaucratic, or democratic, or task-oriented.

A young employee in a bank complained to me: "I entered the lift and there was one of our seniors. I said 'good morning'; not only did he fail to respond, but would not lift his eyes off the newspaper to look at me." The young man uttered his account in sadness and bewilderment. Looking is recognition of a person you encounter, depending of course on how you look. By just looking, you acknowledge the presence of another human being in a space you and he share. Don't misunderstand me; I am not asking that we should be indiscriminately passionate and solicitous. People I surveyed do not like a boss to be too soft, loving, spineless, or angelic. While they expect recognition, they also want to be able to *look up* to a boss. Interestingly, when you look up you assume an upright posture. Self *respect* and respect of the other go hand in hand.

Once while traveling in London, I engaged a taxi driver in a private conversation about his life. It was a long ride. I found out that besides being a taxi driver, he was also an accomplished fisherman. "A true fisherman," he told me, "must have respect for the fish he is trying to catch." To him, fishing is more than winning a battle with the fish. "Fishing," he says, "is a sort of dialogue with your favorite kind of fish." Note that the fisherman does not seek any kind of fish but only his favorite kind. There must be *intimacy* in the exercise. No wonder, often fishermen return to the water the fish they catch. A fisherman is equipped with more than knowledge or skill. He also has feelings.

The fisherman's words evoke the experience of a hunter as described by Castaneda in his book *Journey to Ixtlan*.[7] The wise old Indian teaching Don Juan how to become a hunter:

> "To be a hunter is not just to trap game... A hunter that is worth his salt does not catch game because he sets his traps, or because he knows the routines of his prey, but because he himself has no routines. This is his advantage. He is not at all like the animals he is after, fixed by heavy routines and predictable quirks; he is free, fluid, unpredictable." pp. 74-75

The hunter must be *fluid, and unpredictable.* In other words original and creative. And the wise man goes on:

> "In order to be a hunter you must disrupt the routines of your life. Then he *looks* at his disciple who has done well in hunting: you have done well in hunting. You have learned quickly and now you can *see* that you are like your prey, easy to predict... You have observed the habits of animals in the desert. They eat and drink at certain places, they nest at specific spots, they leave their tracks in specific ways; in fact everything they do can be *foreseen* or *reconstructed* by a good hunter. As I told you before, in my eyes you behave like your prey. All of us behave like the prey we are after. That, of course, also makes us prey for something else. Now, the concern of a hunter, who knows all this, is to stop being a prey himself."
> p. 75 [my emphasis]

The Indian sage ends by a question, "Do you *see* what I mean?" Here again, *looking* is the issue. When you look, you see, you think. I recount these two incidents to show that those who deal with animals must have some knowledge of the animal's nature. Moreover, their connection with the animal is intimate enough to rule out animosity or cruelty. Likewise, I

---

[7] Castaneda, C. (1974). *Journey to Ixtlan: The Lessons of Don Juan.* New York: Pocket Books.

hope that managers dealing with human beings would have an idea about the humanness of the people they deal with. A simple model about what makes us human and different from other creatures may point out the proper way of dealing with them. I will try in this book to offer a simple model. The model does not have to be invented — it is already there if you look carefully at the persons you encounter. I met managers who related to subordinates as serfs. Those managers were not aware that misperception is implicit in their conduct.

It is futile to demand a complete theory of the human nature. There are as many theories as there are philosophers and social scientists. It is more urgent and more realistic, I dare say, to have a clear conception of the human individual whom we encounter day on and day out in the course of our life. *Nature* of humankind is too abstract and too remote from the individuals that we meet in our daily existence.

Humanness of the person is an important issue whether we are dealing with a leader, a follower, or a peer. They are all equal and should be considered equal as far as humanness is concerned. A leader, notwithstanding his or her stature does not shed humanity the minute he or she ascends to a leadership position. Nor does the follower lose his humanness simply because he or she ranks low in the social hierarchy. It follows that we ought to bear in mind that some actions taken by a leader could be explained better by reference to his being human rather than to being a holder of leadership position.

The first thing you must be aware of is the fact that you manage a human person, not a person *with* personality. Personality is an integrative concept. In the psychology literature, the role of personality theory is to fill in the existing gulf between the biological and the sociological on one hand and the psychological on the other hand. At this point, I am compelled to ask myself a serious question; *What does it mean to be human? More specifically, what is so distinctive about being human?* First I would like to ensure that we understand what we mean by the term *distinctive*. By distinctive, I mean serving to distinguish a human person from other living creatures.

In my seminars and graduate courses, I try to elicit answers to these questions from my audience. I ask if there is an engineer, or a veterinarian, or a botanist in the audience. I often find one or the other. If so, I ask the vet, "What is the difference between a cow and a human being?" I ask the engineer, "What is the difference between a machine and a human being?" I ask the botanist, "What is the difference between a tree and a human being?" I never failed to get expressions of surprise from the audience, presumably at the strangeness of my questions. Usually however, the audience is amused by a question they may have never posed to themselves. Indeed, they may never have heard. More often than not, I fail to get a satisfactory answer that includes what is distinctive about the human being.

Respondents know of course there is a difference, but they are hardly able to articulate it. A vet may cover up his inability to tell what is distinctive by giving a facetious answer such as "The cow has four legs" to which I say, facetiously as well, "A chicken has two legs. Does this make a chicken similar to a human being?" A botanist once went on lecturing about the process of growth. I interrupted, "Yes we know all this, but in what way is a human different?" After a moment of silence, the botanist replied, "A tree is fixed in place, but a human person is free to move." At this point the audience seems to be thinking together. Initially the audience laughed. The laughter indicates the audience did not apprehend the enormous implication of an animal being able to move freely in the space available — freedom, more space for exploratory behavior, more options, which translates more mastery. But still mobility is not specific to the human person. It does not qualify as distinctive feature distinguishing the human from other species. So we must wait to return to the question to answer it fully. The initial frivolous reactions and amusement give way to serious thinking. Often I get answers that reflect the respondents' immersion in the subject matter of their discipline. People in these disciplines know that there are differences, but knowledge is not enough. Managers must be clear about the implications of their knowledge and bring the knowledge to bear upon the human beings they are in charge of.

MODEL PARAMETERS

I present below, a model of five basic properties that make a human person stand out as a total entity in the face of the world. To my knowledge, these properties have been referred to in literature, but they occurred to me in the course of my life as first-hand experience. Moreover, I bring them together as an integrated whole and show first, how they relate to each other and second, their implications to the human condition. They answer directly the question: *What is distinctive about a human person*. The answer includes the following basic distinctive properties of a human being:

a.   Bio-psycho-social system

b.   A continuous process of becoming

c.   Endowed with the power of talking and use of symbols

d.   Able to assume *upright posture* (UP)

e.   Environmental force

BIO-PSYCHO-SOCIAL SYSTEM

By *system* I mean an organized whole. This implies complexity, differentiation of parts that are interrelated, and integrated into the whole. An individual though small in size by comparison to a corporation or any other large group, is still a system of enormous complexity. Any individual is a pivot of a whole network of relationships. It follows that calling him or her a universe would not be an exaggeration at all.

The biological dimension brings in the body in which an individual resides and by which he or she moves in the world. The human person is immersed in *mother nature* through the biological entity we call *body*. The living body is not just a physical mass. It becomes a physical mass after death, which we rightly call *remains* of the *deceased* person. The body relates the whole person to the physical world, the world of matter, mass, natural elements, things, people, and other creatures. The human body is separate from its surroundings. The apparent separateness is evident as long as we apprehend the body as physical mass. But we cannot ignore the physiological processes going on as long as the person is alive. Its core property is that it is alive. Sensory apparatus allows the person to scan the environment and respond accordingly. Sensory input does not stop even during sleep. Sometimes, the person seeks sensory information, at other times sensory information intrudes coercively into the organism. Regulation of sensory information is the person's effort to maintain his or her integrity in the face of the onslaught of environmental input. Then there is the skin. The skin has the double function of a boundary: separating the whole and at the same time relating the whole to the natural world. Montagu's work is very enlightening.[8] Montagu lists the functions of the skin as follows:

1. Protects the underlying parts from mechanical and radiation injuries, and invasion of foreign substances and organisms

2. Provides the organism with vital sensory information about such matters as temperature, solidity and softness of objects, taste of food, and size (in the absence of visual information)

3. Regulates body temperature

4. The skin is involved in the metabolism and storage of fat, and in water salt metabolism by perspiration

5. Serves as a reservoir of food and water

6. Facilitates the two-way passage of gases through it; and

7. Acts as the seat of the origin of the anti-rachitic vitamin D

The body is simultaneously part of the objective world (nature) and the subjective world (self). Being a part of the objective world, the body is subject to natural forces — temperature, light, humidity, and the like.[9]

---

[8] Montagu, A. (1978). *Touching: The Human Significance of the Skin.* New York: Harper & Row.
[9] Straus, E. (1963). *The Primary World of Senses: A vindication of sensory experience.* Transl. J. Needleman. New York: The Free Press, Glencoe, Illinios.

The body is a vehicle of transportation we call mobility. The body is endowed with tremendous potential to develop skills which are intimately connected to sensation, motivation, emotionality and cognition. Physical skills are guided by cognitive processes of perception, reasoning, imagination and memory processes. We may extend the power of the body beyond muscular skill since as we know from biology that the power of thinking and other high mental faculties rests on the health of the body.

It is not odd, therefore, to call the living body a *physical self*. It is the means whereby we present our SELF to the world. The curious thing is that the human body as a living entity is more able than the human person to protect its identity. It rejects a foreign body and manages the process of exchange in the most effective way, provided we don't interfere. Furthermore, we cannot talk about work motivation without recognizing the role of physical endurance in perseverance and dedication.

The Social Dimension

The human person's identity is achieved through a long process of socialization. The individual is human to the extent that he or she participates in social institutions. He or she occupies various positions or assumes a variety of roles within a given social matrix. We should be able to recognize that the individual has a place in the world. We should relate to him or her as an active participant in the common drama of humanity. There is a great deal of information about the social activities of exchange with other people as individuals or groups. But the relation between the physiological and the social remained curiously ignored. In fact physiological processes could not be fulfilled by the individual except through interaction with other agents. George Herbert Mead (1967) points out that all social interrelations and interactions are rooted in a certain common socio-physiological endowment of every individual. These physiological bases of social behavior are such, precisely because they in themselves are also social. They are mechanisms which necessarily involve more than one individual. As George Herbert Mead (1934) notes, physiological activities in sexuality, parenting, and in attacks and defenses are social in that the acts begun within the organism require their completion in the actions of others. As Mead noted, while the pattern of the individual act may be said to be in these cases social, it is only so in so far as the organism seeks the stimuli in the attitudes and characters of other forms for the completion of its own responses, and by its behavior tends to maintain the other as a part of its own environment.

That the psychological and biological are inseparable shows in the role of the body in interpersonal communication. I am referring specifically to the crucial importance of non-verbal communication such as facial expressions, gestures, movement of the hand, mimics, smiles and motor behavior.

A CONTINUOUS PROCESS OF BECOMING

Personality is a process of becoming. Becoming is implicit in the process of natural maturation.[10] Becoming proceeds in a natural fashion. It is irreversible, a flux towards the future, towards what is yet to become. It is beyond our control. We cannot change the order or sequence. We cannot, for example, get the infant to change the order of teeth development or verbal development. We may try to accelerate either but our intervention is often destructive. We can only create the conditions that facilitate the natural maturation. Natural maturation, orderly as it is, does not proceed in a uniform or smooth fashion. It includes surges that have clear features of developmental crises — teething, puberty, menopause, and ageing. Each of these crises demands both self management and need for societal support and understanding.

---

[10] I define personality as a set of potentialities that emerge in time in response to diverse circumstances. Potentialities emerge in accordance with the process of organic maturation. A healthy environment provides the individual with the care and the learning opportunities that enhance the maturational process. Smooth maturation is contingent on the deliberate exercise of the skills and abilities pertaining to a given maturational phase. Maturation is spurred by practice, trial and error, experimentation, and social inducement. (Quote from Alexandria paper)

Emergence of Language

When the speech organs and concept formation reach a certain level of maturation, the child sets on acquiring the language of his/her folks. Language makes us different from other animals. It is then that physical handling of the child is replaced by verbal communication. We request or demand, cajole or intimidate, persuade or coerce, all through the medium of words. Sometimes, our words fail to get the child's compliance, so we reach for the cane, thus regressing to physical coercion. The older the child is, the more intervention is required on behalf of a social agent, be it a parent or a parent surrogate, or a teacher, or even a policeman. Biological maturation of the child is met with parallel change in the behavior of adults towards the child. In other words, the process of socialization involves both the child and social agents. Therefore socialization is not a one-way process.

Unfolding of Potentialities

The concept of becoming has important theoretical underpinning. It implies that the future of the human person is not determined exclusively by their past but also by the future they envision. What they have done in the past and continue to do at present does not define them. There is much more they can do and learn to do. However, we must realize that there is no such thing as *the future*. There is only the future which we chart for ourselves. Actualities are not sufficient to determine the future we envision. Potentialities must be considered. Potentialities unfold in time in reaction to societal and environmental demands, given proper learning and opportunities for growth. The roles we assume in various social systems will determine which potentialities will be activated and which will remain dormant. Human capacity for learning is enormous. Rarely do we find the time or opportunity to exploit them fully or optimally.

Thus, becoming implies that personality is never a finished entity at any time in the person's history. Nature decided that human infancy lasts longer than any animal infant. This is because animals are equipped by instinct, a natural program that emerges soon after birth. Nature equipped the human infant with a complex brain, an open system that allows a myriad of alternative avenues for growth. Being an open system, the human brain endows the child with enormous potentialities of adaptation. This maximizes the role of learning and together with it, the need for society to intervene, that is, to complement nature's role. This places a heavy burden on society to devise child rearing practices until the child is ready to set out on his or her own.

The process of becoming takes place in the context of a social system. In the course of one's life, a person joins multiple social systems. Membership is the vehicle whereby the individual's history merges with the history of one or the other of social systems. In modern times the career of a single individual is time-bound. Cultural values determine the degree to which a person's life is bound by the history of a single social system. Becoming proceeds until the finishing line.

Becoming and Time Experience

One might object to becoming as a distinctive feature of the human person since all living creatures are also in the process of becoming. After all, being alive means being constantly changing according to a predetermined program which unfolds in time. However, humans are historical creatures. They are conscious of time passing, they anticipate and plan. They record history and make their own future. They live the present guided by a past and with an eye on the future, theirs and that of their offspring. Furthermore, our mode of existence in the present time implies looking ahead, entertain aspirations and hopes. This means that future orientation determines the mode of existence in the here and now. The relationship between the present and the future is dialectic. We cannot separate them from each other in our consciousness.

Alfred Korzybski's (1974)[11] states that humanity is a class of life distinctly different from animals because only humans can pass on

---

[11] Korzybski, A. (1974). *Manhood of Humanity* (first published 1931), pp. 9–111 and 186.

recorded knowledge from one generation to the next. Stressing continuity from one generation to the next Korzybski states that the next generation does not need to reinvent the wheel. The previous generation gives to the new generation its accumulated knowledge as well as its material goods. This is how civilizations develop.

ENDOWED WITH THE POWER OF TALKING AND USE OF SYMBOLS

In my teaching, I like to define leadership as *The art of talking with the intent to influence.* I never fail to get protestations from the audience, "How about non-verbal communication?" I usually respond, "A human being is in the first place a talker." Talking is our primary tool of communication if we want anything done by others or with others. Talking is always in the forefront of communication. After all, illiteracy does not prevent us from talking. In my childhood in Egypt I met women who were able to read but could not write. Why only women? This is because traditionally women were not allowed school education beyond puberty. Once puberty sets in, tradition required young girls to move to a phase of premarital training preparing them for their future role as household managers. A common sight in villages in Egypt is a man reading a newspaper to a group of other men, presumably illiterate, sitting in a semi circle around the reader and listening intently to what he reads.

Hobbes asserted that "the most noble and profitable invention of all other, was that of SPEECH." Without speech, adds Hobbs, "there would have been amongst men neither commonwealth, nor society, nor contract, nor peace, no more than amongst lions, bears and wolves."[12] Going further back in history "The way to truth," says Plato, "is not writing, but dialectics, that is the spoken word with its implications of two, or rather three parties: the speaker, the listener and the language they share."[13] Aristotle refers to man's *power of speech.* According to Aristotle, speech is

---

[12] Smith, T. V., & Greene, M. (Eds.). (1970). *From Descartes to Locke.* Chicago: The University of Chicago Press.
[13] Quoted by Safouan, p. 72.

what makes a human a political animal. Aristotle has this to say about the power of speech:

> "But obviously man is a political animal in a sense in which a bee is not, or any other gregarious animal, Nature, as we say, does nothing without some purpose; and she has endowed man alone among the animals with the power of speech. Speech is something different from voice, which is possessed by other animals also and used by them to express pain or pleasure; for their nature does indeed enable them not only to feel pleasure and pain but to communicate these feelings to each other. Speech, on the other hand serves to indicate what is useful and what is harmful, and so also what is just and what is unjust. For the real difference between man and other animals is that humans alone have perception of good and evil, just and unjust, etc. It is the sharing of a common view in these matters that makes a household and a state." p. 60

THE UPRIGHT POSTURE

I worked with a schizophrenic patient for three years. I discovered in the course of therapy that whenever he was in a depressed mood, he would walk slowly, the head and shoulders bowed forward. As a result, his field of vision does not extend much beyond his feet. To remain in this posture for long, the patient must feel claustrophobic and consequently depressed. It occurred to me to get him make an effort to set his sight far away from the spot of space he occupied. I would encourage him to look through the window at the trees that extend far away in the distance and report what he sees. I urged him to *really look actively, not just receive passively.* I got him to look up at the sky and report the different colors of the clouds, the trees, and flowers. Soon enough with the flow of various sensory input into his consciousness, the depressive mood subsides and the patient would become less lethargic and more communicative.

Looking straight ahead, as an act of will, brings the third dimension into our awareness. One is no more a prisoner of a narrow space. At the time I conducted this experiment with the patient, I was not aware that the exercise compelled the patient to recover the upright posture. How else could the patient be able to look as far as possible? Since then, this phenomenon became an important item to observe in my work with patients both in diagnosis and psychotherapy. In teaching the psychology of perception, I call the ability to stand up *triumph of humankind over gravity.* I used to drop a heavy object which falls to the ground with a bang. Then I tell the audience, "This is what is natural. The fact that I maintain the upright position is an act of will. We *should not take it for granted lest we lose it.*" And we actually lose it whenever we grow discouraged, fatigued or helpless.

I found out later that this feature was already known to Erwin Straus, an eminent psychiatrist and philosopher. The Upright Posture occupied a central position in his philosophical doctrine. I was thrilled to find out, at last, that what I had arrived at as a personal experience had solid scientific backing. Erwin Straus' earlier specialty was anatomy. Straus goes into great detail in showing that the upright posture is determined by the anatomical properties of the human body linking the structural features to the purpose of the upright posture.

> "Upright posture, while unique, is also essential. This is no necessary consequence. The exceptional might be nothing but a peculiarity, an accidental caprice of nature. However, there is no doubt that the shape and function of the human body are determined in almost every detail by, and for, the upright posture. The skeleton of the foot; the structure of the ankle, knee, and hip; the curvature of the vertebral column; the proportions of the limbs — all serve the same purpose. This purpose could not be accomplished if the muscles and the nervous system were not built accordingly." p.156

ENVIRONMENTAL FORCE

As soon as you make an appearance in a social situation, you will impact others. People do not wait for you to do or to say anything. Whether you talk or remain silent, a certain perception accompanied by emotive reaction is inevitable. Being a social force implies that you have the power to impact others, but also the powerlessness to determine how you will be perceived by others. People will react to your presence. Their reaction will depend on the extent to which you are aware of your inherent power to influence others by your very presence. Observers' reaction may be either positive (in your favor), negative (oppositional) or neutral (dismissive). Your presence may be insignificant to the extent that people *learn* to ignore you as long as you remain inconsequential. This means your social impact will depend on the way you *manage* your relationships in a given field. If you ignore the fact that you are an environmental force and fail to utilize this property, people will guess and form random judgments about you. It is important that you carry the burden of defining yourself. You must establish *presence* wherever you are. It has just occurred to me that the word *present* has two meanings: one is *here and now;* the other meaning is a *gift*. Could it be that establishing presence is a sort of gift for the person and for the group in which the person becomes a member? It is not enough for a person to see himself or herself as environmental force. He or she must ascribe the same quality to every other human.

So far, I stressed the human as an environmental force in relation to other human individuals or human societies. We must also recognize that this force impinges on nature which includes animals, plants, and matter. Humans do not passively accept the physical environment as it is given. They modify it to suit their ends. In other words, human individuals humanize the natural environment. This brings to mind the role of labor and work in defining the nature of the human species. This subject will be dealt with in a later chapter. We must also realize that as you try to change circumstances, you also change in the process. Influence is reciprocal as George Herbert Mead[14] has noted:

"As a man adjusts himself to a certain environment he becomes a different individual; but in becoming a different individual he has affected the community in which he lives. It may be a slight effect, but in so far as he has adjusted himself, the adjustments have changed the type of the environment to which he can respond and the world is accordingly a different world. There is always a mutual relationship of the individual and the community in which the individual lives."

Some individuals have strikingly changed the community. Mead goes on:

"Persons of great mind and great character have strikingly changed the community to which they have responded. We call them leaders, as such, but they are simply carrying to the nth power this change in the community by the individual *who makes himself a part of it, who belongs to it.* The great characters have been those who, by being what they were in the community, made that community a different one. They have enlarged and enriched the community." p. 215 [my emphasis]

Mead stresses the fact that these individuals have been able to effect change in the community by virtue of having become *part of it.* He came very close to the realization that a leader's influence on a given community derives from having been a *member* in that community. In other words, membership is the mechanism which explains a leader's success in changing the group he or she leads. The phenomenon of membership will be dealt with in detail in a later chapter.

---

14 Mead, G. H. (1962). *Man, Self, and Society.* Chicago: The University of Chicago Press (first published 1934).

SYNTHESIS

OLD CONCEPTS THROUGH MY EXPERIENCE

I submitted a minimum number of characteristics that answer the question, *What does it mean to be human?* I limited the characteristics to five distinctive features. I did not invent any of these features. One or the other features has appeared in literature. However, I included them in the book only if they had emerged in my mind to describe my own experience in the course of my professional or personal journey. Initially the five properties characterizing a human person seemed distinct, but it does take much reflection to realize that they are dynamically interdependent. They reveal the reality of the human nature from different perspectives. After all, the human person is too complex to be grasped from a single perspective. It does not really matter which vantage point we start with. We can take any property and soon we will find out that it is intrinsically connected with one, or more, of the other properties. Let us demonstrate by some examples.

Take the concept of the *upright posture*. In the first place, the upright posture was made possible by the anatomical structure of the human body as Straus has shown. Anatomical structure of the body made it possible for the human to resist gravity. As such, the upward posture is a dynamic state signifying the person's readiness to mobilize the potential energy to bounce him or her into the world. In other words, a human is endowed with the ability to stand up in the presence of others *and be counted*. Maintaining the upright posture is a prerequisite for establishing presence in the world. It is also a strong signal of readiness to participate, resist, or confront. The best reply to an insulting gesture from an insensitive and arrogant person is to stand erect, look straight at him or her. There would be no need to utter a word. It is then that silence sounds louder than shouting. However, this potentiality is realized given the will which could be defeated by a serious physical or mental disorder. It may also be aborted under duress such as when one is threatened by a powerful enemy.

THE UPRIGHT POSTURE AND COGNITION

The upright position stirs up cognition through the expansion of the visual field. When standing, you do not look at your feet but cast your sight away from the location which your body occupies. Thus, sensory horizon expands, and varies, as you move forward or sideways or backward. You are then able to move from *here* to *there*. Moving from where you are to a place ahead, a destination, or target, is a movement both in space and time. In other words, expansion of the sensory field is contiguous with expansion of the time horizon. There is no future, as lived experience, unless the focus of attention shifts from the *here* and the *now* to the *there* (space) and the *then* (time). In other words, the ability to maintain an upright posture is prerequisite for the experience of *becoming*.

Becoming as the experience of movement towards a future is only possible given that personality is a set of possibilities that defy, or transcend actualities. Casting your sight away from where you are now, sets the stage for becoming. I am reminded of the story of George Mallory, the English mountaineer who took part in the first two British expeditions to Mount Everest in the early 1920s. Mallory is famously quoted as having replied to the question *Why do you want to climb Mount Everest?* with the statement: "Because it's there." I am aware that there have been questions over the authenticity of that quote. However, whether Mallory had actually uttered these words does not matter given our purpose here. What matters is that he looked up at Mount Everest. And soon enough, Mount Everest, a site on the map, was transformed to a destination Mallory must reach at some time in the future. The forces of becoming were set in motion. Once more, we see sense in Wittgenstein admonition, *Don't think. Just look.*

Seeing a person as a universe with potentialities that unfold in time is a very important feature which should guide our efforts in all fields of endeavor. Concrete thinking limits our mental grasp to what is observable and we may lose sight of what *might* be there, or *could* be realized. Not many managers or teachers exercise enough imagination to go beyond the actual that is witnessed directly. Realization that personality is a set of potentialities releases the forces of becoming. That is what Socrates had realized centuries ago when he likened a teacher to a midwife whose role it is to *draw out* what the person already has but is not aware of. Indeed, that is confirmed by the Latin root of the word Education which is *ex ducere*, or leading out. That is also the basis of artistic creation. A sculptor, for example, would tell you that the statue he erected was already embedded in the mass of rock. Through an imaginative act the sculptor dared to free the *potential* form hidden in the mass of rock. Meanwhile, what the sculptor produced became in turn a social force inspiring present and future onlookers. And yet, becoming does not cut us off from our past. Rather it evokes the past and reinterprets it in a way that enhances the emergence of different modes of existence.

The principle of *becoming* implies that a human being is incomplete at any stage of his or her life. Personality is never a finished product. Incompleteness drives the person to learn, experiment, and alter circumstances — in other words, to exercise his or her potential as a force in the environment. This is sometimes impossible without intervention from social agencies such as in the case of a child or a sick or incapacitated adult. Becoming according to natural maturation spells renewal, unfolding of stages of a predetermined program and according to a certain order and rhythm that should not be violated. For example, we cannot force the emergence of concept formation in a child before the maturation of certain supporting biological functions. There is always a rhythm that varies from one function to the other. But this is becoming predetermined by the biology of the human being. However, our existence is not determined exclusively by biological forces. The will plays a significant part, spontaneity supported by abilities, and moral and legal obligations.

Let us learn a lesson from this regarding the meteoric rise of a young man or woman in a hierarchical social system. There is always negative aftermath if the rise has been forced by shallow ambition and inappropriate circumstances. This is also a common phenomenon in the field of entertainment. Often we see a person achieving stardom in a very short time and in an unexpected way. Usually the end is negative and sometimes catastrophic. There comes the time when the rising star cannot go any further. The same applies to a person who became rich overnight such as when winning a lottery. This phenomenon did not escape the attention of the public reflected by the expression, *nouveau riche*. The suddenness of wealth allows the *nouveau riche* no sufficient time to adjust. Only a person with strong character and solid value system can reorder his or her life and resist the temptation of abuse of the newly earned wealth. The same applies to a mediocre leader regarding sudden access of a position with enormous powers.

We have dealt with the individual as a force in relation to other people. It is important to remember that this force impinges on animals, plants and the physical environment at large. This brings us to the role of human labor and work in the exploitation of natural resources and shaping the environment to become a human *habitat*. We will deal with this subject in a later section of this book. Work and labor demonstrate that humans have formidable ability to contribute to the work of nature. And yet, we should not lose sight that they have equal ability to mess up the work of nature.

INDIVIDUAL DIFFERENCES

We have been talking so far about distinctive features of the human person *in the abstract*. But a person in the abstract does not exist in reality. Only individuals *in flesh and blood* exist. It follows that human beings as individuals or as groups participate in one or the other features in varying degrees. This amounts to saying that humanity is relative. When human persons go wild, they are not able to live as animals do. That is because animals are more guided by instinct than humans. Animals do not assassinate, they eat other animals to survive. They eat when hungry, they drink when thirsty, and they migrate when they have to. There is hunger in animals, but no greed. Animals stop fighting when the *need* for fighting has been satisfied. On the positive side, humans can share in divinity and are capable of self-denial; furthermore, they can aspire towards lofty ideals, and lead spiritual existence.

Dehumanization does not escape our attention when extreme as in the case of serfdom, slavery, or oppression. Torture techniques practiced in Abu Ghraib prison aimed to break the will of the victim and destroy his or her identity as a human being. For example, one victim, a respectable citizen in his community, is forced to take off his clothes, given a lace around his neck, and the torturers would drag him around as a dog. More tragic forms of dehumanization show in treating human persons as inanimate objects — forcing a number of men to lie on top of each other in such a way as to form a pyramid of nude men. Such acts are committed by decadent human beings. Little did the torturers know that they deny their own humanity the very moment they dehumanize other fellow humans.

Our concern here is with subtle forms of dehumanization that may be committed by presumably normal individuals when they take humanism of others as a matter of fact. We are acquainted with huge literature in the annals of psychology and sociology about prejudice. We will not go into that. Suffice it to state that many practices in certain fields violate, albeit with the best of intention, one or more of the features outlined in our model. Let us cite briefly some examples.

• *In Education*

In some circles, the child is considered less human than the adult. It is true that the child is less mature than the adult. It is equally true that he or she is in a continuous state of becoming according to the law of natural maturation. Becoming implies that the human individual is incomplete at all ages. Incompleteness is not an insult when coupled with the drive to become different through tapping of enormous potentialities. It is society's duty to complement incompleteness by adequate socialization practices.

- *In Management*

I would like to ask, or rather challenge, managers if they know about the nature of the human person as much as a veterinary doctor knows about a cow or a dog or a horse. And if they do know, do they treat employees as totally human or as *minimally* human? Maybe we do not know how a person could be treated less than totally human. The roles we assign to people must correspond to what is essentially human. Unfortunatley, education and organizational policies often fail to provide opportunities for individuals to utilize — and develop — their full potential. Ignoring individual differences and treating men and women as undifferentiated mass, ignore the right of each for personal identity. Then there is emphasis on how a person is at a given moment in time and less attention to potentialities which rarely show in a person's contemporary skills. I like to point out that marketing tactics, with its reliance on various social science findings, treat consumers as fair objects of manipulation.

- *In Scientific Psychology*

We sometimes derive conclusions about human beings from experiments conducted on animals. What is more serious is that often experimental animals are not studied in their natural environments, but in artificial environments designed by scientists. This means that experimental animals are robbed of their animal nature. In contrast, scientists in the field of Ethology study animals in their natural habitats. Findings of their studies show animals to have much more potential than we have ever thought. Ethology studies provide hypotheses that shed a great deal of light on human behavior.

- *In Law Enforcement*

The way we treat prisoners: we must condemn their act and they must pay for the crime, but according to the law not more. They are entitled for reform and re-education based on potentialities that have been ignored often due to social rather than individual pathology. I am not arguing in favor of the prison environment to mimic a comfortable resort. Still it must be an environment that responds to legitimate human needs.

- *In Politics*

During the late 19th century, it was common for European intellectuals to compare non-Western 'primitive' adults to European children in characteristics such as natural deficiency in self control, concrete thinking, animistic thinking, inability to comprehend cause-effect relationships, or planning. European colonization of Asia and Africa provided ample opportunities for writers, including scientists in the fields of psychology and anthropology, to create a cultural image which Saïd (1979)[15] called the cultural "Other." The image provided justification not only for colonizing the *primitive* nations but also assuming the *burden* of civilizing them. There was a time when African-American slaves were not considered persons in America, or, at best, ³/₅ of a person. Sadly, we have not always granted the status of person to all human beings.

PRACTICAL IMPLICATIONS

We need to examine the philosophical (and value) underpinnings of our theories and practices in all fields of endeavor. I submit that the properties of humanness outlined above may have great contribution to humanization of our policies and practices. The effect of assimilation of the properties presented in this chapter may not be obvious. Nor can we demand that each attribute we assimilate will affect our behavior directly as the attribute indicates. That does not happen. But assimilation of the whole model will have insidious effect on a person's self concept and his or her perception of the other. It is through perception that behavioral change can take place in an insidious manner.

---

[15] Saïd, E. W. (1979). *Orientalism*. New York: Vintage.

VALUE OF THE MODEL

The reader might consider my stressing the humanity of the human tautological, and therefore trivial. I would say that precisely is the problem. We tend to take it for granted or consider being human obvious enough. Then what is taken for granted is filed away when it comes to actual dealings with human beings. It is taken for granted, but we keep doing things with humans ignoring the primary fact that no matter how imperfect human nature is realized in a person, he or she is still intrinsically human and should be treated as such. I am not referring only to treatment of others, but also to treatment of oneself. Self dehumanization is as serious a fault as dehumanization of others.

APHRODITE
Goddess of love, beauty and sexuality

Harmony envelops the rendering of the female body as an integrated whole. You could not separate any part of the body from the rest. The breasts are not attached to the body. They emerge from the whole. They are like a musical sentence in a symphony. Aphrodite's hand gently touches the breast to express the harmony of feeling with the physicality of the body. The body is presented as a physical self in our world. The artist is telling us, "Don't think, just look." The female body is dignified and venerated. Womanhood is presented as divine.

(Descr.) Aphrodite of the Syracuse type. Parian marble, Roman copy of the 2nd century CE after a Greek original of the 4th century BC; neck, head and left arm are restorations by Antonio Canova. Found at Baiae, Southern Italy. (Current location) National Archaeological Museum, Athens. (Credit) Former Hope Collection; gift by M. Embeirikos, 1924.

CHAPTER THREE

MEMBERSHIP AND ROLE ACQUISITION

A STATE OF BELONGING

When I ask a person, "Where do you work?" The answer I often get is, "I work in such and such organization." The preposition *in* may be interpreted to mean *inside*. It is not the building. It is a collectivity of people that is usually structured in intricate and changing ways. You work inside a room, in an office. But that does not imply that you exist in the organization as an object exists in space. In other words, the organization is not a container. Besides, neither the person nor the organization is an inert entity. Both the organization and the individual are dynamic systems of high degree of complexity, constantly acting, influencing and subject to influence, which means changing. It would therefore be more appropriate to state that the individual exists *in relation to* rather than located *inside* the organization.

What is then the meaning of *being in a relationship* with the organization? The answer is: the individual exists as an active member of the organization. Membership is a mode of existence in relation to any collectivity. Again, *in relation to* does not imply being next to other individuals although proximity is often inevitable. Membership indicates being there with some concern, with some interest, with the intent to exchange with other members and, what is equally important, to have a future, to continue living as a force in the environment beyond the family.

The model of a human person presented earlier implies that the individual *becomes* human through membership in the family, the first social system the individual joins naturally. However, membership in the family is simply a phase in the individual's life history. When the child reaches a certain level of maturity, he or she must seek membership outside the family. The process of *becoming* continues beyond the family sphere.

The average person belongs simultaneously to several social systems. This is a given. It follows that no one could be totally included in a single social system. This amounts to a law governing social living which came to be called, the law of *partial inclusion*. However, the degree and mode of inclusion vary according to the type of the organization, its function in the global environment, and its core values. For example, secret societies require near total inclusion. The military requires total inclusion at least during an initial specified period after which the individual is allowed to commute between the barracks and the outside world.

It is miraculous how a human being manages to synthesize several memberships and still enjoys a unified entity that we call *identity*. A personal incident comes to mind and is worth sharing with the readers. An American psychologist once asked me, "What do you consider yourself: Egyptian, Arab, or Muslim?" I could not then answer the question which sounded rather strange, and may have irritated me a little. The reason for my reaction appears to be that the colleague was not able to deal with me without having a clear definition of who I was to him. I had absolutely no difficulty dealing with him without the need to define him other than being a colleague whom I met in a professional occasion. I needed no information about him other than what he cared to reveal to me. But I will try now to answer his question in the light of the concept of membership. I grew up with the feeling that being Egyptian, Arab and Muslim are not separate. Somehow the three attributes had merged imperceptibly in my personal identity. Which of these comes to the fore depends on how another person presents himself to me. If the other person presents himself to me as a Christian, I would probably remember that I am Muslim. On the other hand, if he tells me that he is American, I would spontaneously invoke my citizenship as Egyptian-American. In the final analysis, my perceived identity in any encounter will be a function of how the other person presents himself to me. The *intrapersonal* is never separate from the *interpersonal*.

MEMBERSHIP: A HISTORICAL PROCESS

Membership is not one event in time. In a formal organization, the process is initiated by search, recruit, and finally all sorts of assessment procedures ending by actual appointment as a member in a given position. Becoming a member, legally speaking, is often followed by training, or indoctrination. Membership may be well structured and standardized in some organizations such as the military. Indoctrination in the military aims at wiping out civilian habits and attitudes. Military values are inculcated to replace civilian values. Indoctrination period is followed by intensive training. Business organizations focus on training in varying degrees and focus less on indoctrination. In other less structured organizations, initiation of membership takes a less structured form such as an orientation session, including the signing of employment contract. The person is then left to his own devices.

Joining a group poses a problem both to the new member and to the group itself. The new member may feel that joining an organization endangers his or her sense of identity — the danger of becoming anonymous, or just a number. Fortunately, the individual does not have to give up entirely his or her identity, nor does he have to become totally anonymous. It is true though that certain groups demand total anonymity such as in fanatic organizations. Rather than giving up one's identity, the individual acquires a fresh identity, through the assumption of roles or functions that have value to the group and agrees somewhat with the member's life goals. Membership is perpetuated by being constantly informed about what is happening to the institution and how it stands relative to other institutions and the world. Members remain members through participation.

A member in the beginning is a novice. Reaction of group members vary in the way the novice is received. The way the novice presents him/herself will determine the way other members will receive him. Appearing too self confident or too meek does not help in the new member's integration. The best approach from a new member is to look, explore, and learn. The new member's experience in former organizations is of little relevance. Becoming a member is a phase requiring from the novice a high degree of sensitivity and social skills.

The fact that membership is a continuous process is indicated by such traditions as emeritus status in universities or in professional organizations. In the USA, once a president was elected, he will be considered president for life beyond his tenure. A former president is given an office, official guards, and is always briefed by the incumbent president of significant decisions and policies. Moreover, he is often called upon to perform duties since he is also a citizen of the country. I must add that the president's membership lasts beyond his life as the tradition of presidential library implies. Thus, life of the former presidents and the history of the country merge. Continuity of membership reflects both continuity and endurance of the organization or the country as a whole. I once visited a Catholic University in the USA where professors are buried on campus — I was greatly moved by the symbolism of perseveration of membership after death. In authoritarian countries of the Third World, nations are deprived of this position of *Former President*. This is because typically presidents do not retire voluntarily. Often a president stays in power until natural death, or assassination.

Membership in any organization limits the member's freedom. Yet it provides opportunities for growth and self-expression. There are aspects in one's personality that will be revealed only in a social setting, namely away from the family. It is important to note that new members are included in the organization through a group, never directly.

Eric Berne (1966)[16] defines membership in terms of the position of the individual to the external boundary of the group to which the individual belongs. Berne states:

> "In some cases, [the individual] finds himself involuntarily and automatically included at birth, as in citizenship and kinship. In other cases it must be crossed inward by such processes as immigration, baptism, initiation, employment, admission or matriculation."

Berne then adds:

> "Withdrawal across the external boundary is known variously by such terms as emigration, resignation or graduation; extrusion across it is called expulsion, excommunication, or discharge; and exclusion is known by such terms as failure or rejection. The major internal boundary is crossed inward by election, succession or appointment and similar processes. Withdrawal from the leadership region occurs through abdication, resignation, retirement or expiration of term; extrusion from it is called variously deposition, demotion, recall, expulsion or removal." p. 57

---

[16] Berne, E. (1966). *The Structure and Dynamics of Organizations and Groups.* New York: Grove Press.

Berne noted that there are more terms for outward crossing of the major internal boundary than for inward crossing. To test Berne's observation I consulted the dictionary and searched all I could find of the terms referring to either outward (exclusion) or inward (inclusion) crossing of boundary. In my search I found a third category not mentioned by Berne, which could not be neatly included in either of Berne's two categories. I gave this category the designation *mixed*. The three categories are shown in the table below.

TABLE: 1

Lexicon of Inclusion and Exclusion

INWARD	OUTWARD		MIXED
admit	dismiss	exile	extradite
hire	fire	strip of citizenship	house arrest
employ	banish	disinherit	isolate
appoint	discharge	disown	ostracize
nominate	expel	eliminate	emigrate
elect	sack	dislodge	demote
naturalize	give the boot	oust	promote
adopt	expel	resign	defect
	mass transfer	retire	outsource
	excommunicate		

Some of the entries in the table above call for further clarification, as shown below.

• *Resignation*

The individual exercises his/her freedom to quit for whatever reasons. This is the only power the individual has over the organization provided resignation occurs voluntarily and is granted. However, even this right is denied in authoritarian regimes where it is common that high ranking officials in government are denied the right of voluntary retirement or resignation. A group of ministers in a Third World country submitted their resignation to the president on account of their disapproval of a given policy. The president turned down their request with the admonition, "I have no ministers who can resign. They can only be fired." And of course the officials withdrew their resignation. In many other authoritarian regimes, high officials do not dare to resign lest their resignation would be interpreted as protest.

- *Emigration*

Emigration may be a voluntary act such as when a member ventures to flee from tyranny of dictatorial regimes, or from oppressive traditions, or simply from pressure for conformity. Often emigration is resorted to in the pursuit of opportunities not available in the emigrants' countries of origin. In a global world this is the phenomenon known by the term *brain drain*, endemic in developing countries such as Egypt. The number of professionals lost to Egypt (as of the year 2009) exceeded 500,000. This estimate is confined to experts in highly advanced scientific and technological fields. Many of these experts hold very sensitive positions in various agencies in the USA alone. Not less serious is the exodus of millions of Egyptian skilled labor serving Gulf countries and other nations in the Arab Middle East. The latter had devastating effect on the quality of daily services to the Egyptian nation.

Let us now turn to the conditions presented in the third column of the table, starting by the two opposing terms, *promote* and *demote*. The issue here is not outward crossing but internal mobility, upward and downward respectively. The opposing terms reflect the sanctioning power of the organization according to bureaucratic criteria. That is assuming the organization is devoid of nepotism or any other forms of corruption.

- *House Arrest, Isolate and Ostracize*

These three terms have one feature in common — they are punitive measures exercised by the institution often in violation of civil liberties. Members remain in the fold of their respective groups but are punished or marginalized severely. They become virtual prisoners. Some authoritarian regimes resort to these as a measure of control. In some fanatic groups, and sometimes religious sects these punitive measures are usually rationalized as reform.

- *Extradition*

Extradition is a case of two-way crossing, emigration interrupted by forced return to country of origin, presumably a legal action.

In conclusion, the contents of the table attest to the richness of the concept of membership. It could be considered a research tool for the study of the intricacies of the attitudes towards membership in formal organizations or in different cultures. I limited the discussion to a few insights of my own. I trust the readers may find many more.

The Familiar Stranger

Anyone who appears in the same context as that of a group will acquire, by necessity the status of *familiar stranger*. The individual acquires some affinity. So sooner or later, he or she will become a fixture in the same environment. I recall going to a certain cafeteria early in the morning. At the same time a number of clients are regular. Sooner or later, we exchange greetings. No other contacts outside. But once we meet somewhere else, we shake hands as if to acknowledge a personal relationship. This is an interesting phenomenon. It proves that nobody remains a stranger for long.

ROLE ACQUISITION

The concept of membership is a very general definition of individuals who participate in the life of any social system irrespective of the type and quality of participation. The concept does not differentiate among members with regard to modes of participation — the concept denotes what people have in common ignoring differences in the mode of existence of different members in the same social system. It is as if members are like atoms milling around randomly in an empty space. A social system has a structure within which members' participation must fit into this structure. In other words each member exists in the organization in a certain capacity. So membership in any social system is usually defined in terms of roles. Group survival and effectiveness depend on the capacity of its members to assume distinct roles. Roles allow individuals to express their individuality in the service of the group. So the notion of membership is an insufficient portrayal of reality. It must be complemented by the concept of role.

A role does not only refer to an enduring position or function one performs in a given social system. Wherever we go in daily life, we find ourselves involved in performing a role: guest or host; superior, co-worker, or subordinate; guide or follower; teacher or student; doctor or patient; sales person or customer; defendant or plaintiff; driver, passenger, or pedestrian; and so on and so forth. Permanent or transitory, a role determines what conduct is appropriate to a specific social setting. In other words, *the role is the frame within which we function*. It is important to realize that a role is a *relational notion*. It describes the expected mode of participation of any member in relation to other holders of different roles in a given situation. It prescribes a dynamic process of exchange between parties, whether individuals or groups. Exchange takes place at three levels:

a. *Responsibility* or the activities a member must perform, is expected to perform, fulfilling obligation, offering product or service;

b. *Authority*, the right, or the power, to make demands on another party, and expecting the latter to comply or cooperate;

c. *Accountability*, the role holder exercises the prerogatives of the position in accordance with law, procedures, or customs. Accountability implies that the role holder is subject to questioning from a higher authority. In the absence of such authority, the role holder is accountable to his community or to him/herself. The latter is what we call moral obligation.

___

FIGURE: 1

Role and Personality

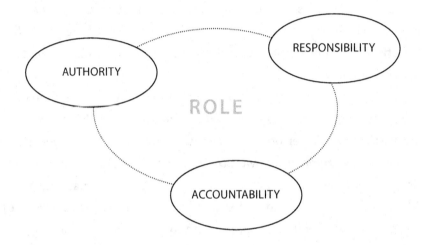

Role Perception
Being a relational notion, role clarity paves the way for sound relationship. In social encounters we often act on the assumption that we know *who we are* in this or that situation to other parties. More seriously, we assume that the other persons know who we are to them. A sound relationship does not proceed on assumptions. Clear perception of our role brings order to our transactions but does not guarantee compatibility unless the other understands our role as we define it to ourselves. In the final analysis we carry the double burden of defining our role to ourselves and define it to whoever we interact with. Social adjustment requires both conditions. Role definition must be in terms of the three components I referred to above namely, *responsibility, authority,* and *accountability*. In any social encounter with another person three questions must be answered clearly:

- What business you have with that person, or what are you expected to offer or receive from him or her (responsibility)?

- What rights are accorded to you, and the same with the other person (authority)?

- To whom would you resort in a case of conflict, who is the person you resort to to resolve the issues over which you conflict (accountability)?

Social Roles and Self Definition

The concept of role is indispensable for understanding the human person as he or she interacts with others in various social situations and institutions. Through a role, a person's inner dynamics flow into behavior in real life situations. At the same time, external demands impact the role holder and find its way into his/her *inner* being. In performing a role, the incumbent's character inevitably colors his or her performance. Sense of identity is sharpened to the extent to which a person is free to choose his roles and manage to orchestrate them in the light of a unifying definition of oneself. This is what I mean by my earlier assertion that *personality is nothing other than a set of potentialities that unfold in time through learning and that makes 'becoming' possible*. What if the role is incompatible with the incumbent's character make up? In such eventuality, the incumbent manifests typical defense mechanisms to minimize damage to his or her integrity. In other words, a minimum of compatibility must exist between role demands and personal inclinations. Clarity about who you are is impossible unless you become clear about the roles you assume in various social settings. The roles you assume willingly and wholeheartedly reflect your core identity, but they also contribute to further development of the identity. This implies that your identity is not, and should not, be frozen in time. Role definition represents the individual's attempt to structure his or her life in a social setting. Role definition is a reflection of the person's ability to adapt to reality demands with optimum satisfaction of the need for autonomy. In this sense, role definition is a mechanism of *becoming*. Clarity of roles minimizes tension and facilitates human interaction. It is much easier to resolve conflict in formal organizations than in informal organizations. This is because roles in formal organizations tend to be formalized, meaning spelled out. And yet there will always be room for subjective interpretation of roles outside technical sectors of a bureaucracy.

A Job Entails Many Roles

A job or a position assigned to a member in any formal system is a complex assignment that entails a minimum of three roles — subordinate, peer, and boss. I might add that while a manager is a member of a specific group, he or she is simultaneously a member of the larger institution within which the immediate group is a sub-system interdependent with other sub-systems. Furthermore, the manager may also be called upon to serve in all sorts of transitory committees or task forces. Leading a unit may entail a great deal of exchange with other units in the same organization or with external organizations. Thus, membership in the global institution confers on the manager what I like to call *representational role*. This is a unique attribute of a manager. While being a member of a group, he or she is the only member that represents the global system within a given unit. In a way, the representational function justifies the manager's authority status within a given unit.

I stated earlier that a formal position has a core of duties or functions related to the mission of the organization. The position engenders multiple social roles. The most pertinent is the triadic constellation we designate, *superior, peer, subordinate*. Contradictions are inherent in any formal position. Resolving the contradictions requires a good deal of sensitivity and social skills. The issue therefore is not leadership but the exercise of influence with a great deal of wisdom people may call *emotional intelligence*. Often the employee is often called upon in addition to fulfilling his/her technical function, to serve on special purpose committees. The situation becomes even more complex when we think that any member of the organization may feel obligated to assume a purely social role that has nothing to do with his or her formal function, such as mediation in case of conflict or providing emotional support or guidance to a subordinate or colleague in distress. After all, no human is an island. He or she is a universe of potentialities only a fraction of which is deployed in the technicalities of any formal job.

Identification

Membership is a relationship that develops between the member and the group, and through the group, with the total institution. The relationship starts as a legal contract, namely utilitarian exchange of benefits. A purely formal relationship does not engage the member's affective needs. Membership as experience is enhanced by participation and assumption of significant roles in the organization. That is when the relationship evolves from a legal binding to a personal bond referred to in the literature as identification. It is then that the member experiences some compatibility between the roles he/she plays in the institution and his or her personal life as a whole. Being a member then becomes an integral part of the person's life project. Identification constitutes a cardinal move in self concept from a *salaried* employee, to use the French expression, to a worthy player in the life of a community.

We must look at multiple memberships as a hierarchy that orders memberships according to the degree and type of members' identification with the social systems in which they are members and in the light of the roles they play. For example, medical personnel identify more closely with the medical profession than with the institution where they happen to practice. This is because their allegiance to their medical profession is more significant, and more compelling, than their membership in the institutions where they practice. For some workers, membership in a labor union may be more or less important than membership in the firm. In less developed societies membership in a formal organization can hardly compete with membership in a primary group such as a family, a tribe, or even a village. Often an official's position in a formal organizational role clashes with his or her role in the primary group such as a family or community. The problem arises when the official is pressured to use his authority within the organization to serve a relative or the community at the expense of the interest of the employer. The pressure is problematic to the extent that identification with the formal and personal systems is equally strong. There seems no easy solution to this problem, so endemic in less developed countries without raising the level of public education.

We often witness that competition exists between citizenship [membership in the nation] and membership in the political party. A politician who belongs to a particular political party must be able to transcend this membership when it comes to decisions affecting the nation. Once elected to the presidency of a country, a politician will be expected to rise above his/her allegiance to the party and identify with the country at large. Election to the presidency gives the politician the legitimate authority to govern the whole entity and devote him/herself totally to the welfare of all citizens.

I should point out at this point that identification should not be confused with absolute loyalty. Otherwise, identification would amount to fascism or fanaticism which in turn will lead to dogmatism. Identification should not stifle the member's critical attitude towards management practices and readiness to provide feedback to those who lead the organization at any level. In other words, what is needed is reasoned identification (see Appendix: Social Structures).

We should bear in mind that individuals do not relate directly to the total organization. They become members in the organization through primary work groups. In due course they join a variety of informal groups from which they learn much about the organization. Members' experience in groups, whether formal or informal, mediates their ultimate attitudes towards the organization. These attitudes are not fixed. Several forces help shape the newcomer's experience:

First, *the immediate supervisor's effort to integrate the newcomer into the organization as a contributing agent.* Unfortunately often supervisors tend to be more superior-oriented than subordinate-oriented. Typically, most of their time and effort is devoted to meeting the demands of their superiors. Supervisors may also be more organization-oriented than subordinate-oriented such as when they appear to be more solicitous of the organization at the expense of the welfare of their immediate subordinates. This state of affairs, I believe, is responsible for the prevalence of two deficiencies in many organizations — inadequate supervision and near absence of apprenticeship.

Second, *peers play a significant role in shaping the newcomer's concept of, and attitude towards, the organization.* Relationship among peers could be cooperative, competitive, or adversarial. Management style of group leaders tips the balance in favor of one or the other of such outcomes. Often healthy relationship among peers compensates for the weakened relationship with the immediate boss. I have been told by several professionals in more than one organization that despite the remoteness of the immediate boss, they would not leave the organization thanks to their *inspiring co-workers.*

Third, *members' identification with their respective groups depends on the perceived status of these groups within the organization.* Groups vary as to their attitudes towards the organization and towards each other. Groups are often in conflict with the organization or at least ambivalent in their attitudes towards the organization. Presthus (1978)[17] challenges the human relations view which defines the organization as *cooperative system* composed of many intimate work groups which meet individual needs for identification. He notes:

> "While small groups undoubtedly meet such needs, it seems equally clear that their members do not necessarily identify with the larger organization. With rare exceptions, the influence of any given individual on this level is inconsequential, and he knows it. As the Hawthorne studies found, the small group often plays a *protective* role, shielding its members from real or imaginary threats of management. Small group relations are often compensatory and negative;

[17] Presthus, R. (1978). *The Organizational Society* (revised edition). New York: St. Martin's Press.

they may even underscore the employee's estrangement from the larger organization. A study of the automobile industry concludes: 'When the worker discussed his relations with other workers and reported social interaction, such as joking, gossiping, or general conversation, he mentioned them chiefly as a fortunate *counterbalance and compensation* for the disliked features of his job.'" p. 201

Fourth, *organization policies and managerial practices convey directly or indirectly something about the employee's worth.*

Fifth, *public image of the organization influences the member's identification with it.* Members may derive pride or shame depending on how the organization is perceived by other organizations or by the public at large. Somehow members like to be affiliated to an organization which is perceived as a respectable institution.

Decline of Identification

In modern times, identification with the organization has been greatly diminished or totally replaced by a contractual obligation based on the price system. In other words, membership may be sustained on the basis of economic necessity. Several factors contribute to this state of affairs:

1. *Elitism:* The organization's increased reliance on technocratic expertise, which may give rise to rampant elitism. Airline pilots may consider themselves the core of aviation industry forgetting that flying a plane is made possible by efforts of various groups on the ground. Doctors may assign more weight to the medical role than the nursing role. In financial institutions, investment experts may regard themselves more relevant than say 'back office' workers. The academic staff in a university may look down at the administrative staff. Elitism is endemic in most modern organizations. And in its extreme form, elitism gives rise to the phenomenon of *inverse identification* — elite groups expecting the organization to identify with them rather than the other way round.

2. *Labor Unions:* Membership in labor unions competes with membership in the organization. Often several competing unions pervade the same organization.

3. *Mergers and Acquisitions:* The wave of mergers and acquisitions has devastating effect on the experience of long-term affiliation.

4. *Globalization:* Globalization transfers power from states to multinational corporations.

5. *Outsourcing:* Outsourcing is a movement that has serious implications as far as membership is concerned. One of the implications may be that corporations grow weary of membership. For them it would be economically advantageous to reduce the volume of membership. This is at variance with the traditional value of loyalty (high degree of identification) with the social system, or the concept of family.

Thus far, we dealt with the issue of identification in general terms. However, since identification is by definition a matter of personal experience, only accounts from individuals would give us a clear idea about the complexity and variability of identification in the life of a member in flesh and blood, as it were. Identification as experience is never that simple. It is highly differentiated, changeable, and often replete with contradictions. I shall give few examples below.

In a counseling session, a young manager confided to me:

> "My working experience and qualification can either bring me everywhere or nowhere. There is no focus. I hope I will be able to create a niche for myself, along with my language skills. I fought hard to get to where I am today, not through aggressiveness or unreasonable demands but through voicing out what I want. I was challenged to take on some new roles. I hope I will be able to surmount these challenges. I do not work in a nurturing environment where mentors keep a lookout for us. Instead we are thrown into the deep end of the pool and left to fight for our own survival."

Note the manager's use of the term, *niche*. It reflects a strong need for intimacy which she finds lacking. The desire for intimacy could be satisfied at a professional level in such behavior as *nurturing* and mentoring.

The experience of another employee betrays the onset of dis-identification or estrangement:

> "I do not wish to see myself in [current job] for long. My personal beliefs do not fit into the organization's culture, it has been a struggle. Of course, I have toughened and learnt a lot in these 3 years with [current employer]. Any longer, I might be swallowed by the harshness of the environment and fade away into the culture."

Another employee laments the fact that she has 'lost herself in the job':

> "My emotions surged after reading an article in the [newspaper] by my favorite journalist. She [the journalist] contributes her thoughts on issues that are close to the nation's heart. Her articles are simple, endearing and always set me thinking. The article today led me to reflect on how much I have lost myself to this job, my energy is drained and my sense of self-confidence is shaken. The payback does not seem to justify this sacrifice. Of course, all is not so negative, I still have a group of great friends, colleagues and family to bring me back to the real world."

A third employee who had already decided to resign from the current employer to join another employer commented:

> "I feel that it is not healthy for me to stay on in an environment where you are made to feel unwanted, unappreciated and whatever you do always falls short of the required standard. It is by God's grace that I have the courage to take this bold step to venture out of my comfort zone for the unknowns ahead. Some colleagues were not surprised, looking at the recent

development. But some were surprised at my courage to give it all up (job, pay, and status). To be honest, I am not sure if regrets will set in later in life. But at this stage, it is a necessary step for self preservation. It was a long struggle for close to a year. Well, whatever it is now, it is time to look ahead..."

All the factors sited above could now be easily discerned in the case of a single subordinate. To illustrate, I quote a first line supervisor who had a rather unfavorable relationship with her immediate boss.

"I have to admit that the constant restructuring and the brutal dismissal of colleagues around me upset me and makes me feel uncertain. Before we can settle into our new role or learn to work with our new team members, we hear of another restructuring. Luckily I still have a group of nice and supportive colleagues."

Interestingly, even when the subject of the session is reporting about her relationship to the boss, she shifted attention to the organization as a whole. When she did, I deliberately tried to steer her back to the original complaint about her boss. I asked, "How does the boss treat you?" She replied, "She is friendly and nicer to me now." She then added a qualification, "I don't know why this change, but I feel worried. This is a big difference from her previous self. I don't mean to be cynical, but it seems like something bad is going to happen to me... Meanwhile, I am on an active lookout for a more suitable career." She then went on to describe the current and future pressure of work:

"After looking through this year's schedule, it was clear that my workload would double as compared to last year. For an equal amount of hard work and increasing politics in the office, I think I could get a better paying job elsewhere. I will not miss my bosses, work and pay. Friends will be missed but new friendship can be built overtime. I have worked with bosses who think I am competent and hardworking, so I think I am not that bad after all. More importantly, I think I am still young so I should take the risk and explore. At this moment, I am just working very hard without knowing what I am doing or where I can move on from here, I am beginning to worry for my future. The only drawback if I leave [my current employer] is the comfort and security of a familiar environment. But then, changes come very often, I cannot see what is coming up next and I am losing motivation, this I think is very bad."

CASE STUDY

Betrayed by the Management

"I am a salesman working for a container company, a family-owned and family-managed firm which manufactures steel and tin containers, with sales close to $100 million per year. The company is tightly structured and I have always felt that rigidity in the sales department. While nobody forces specific rules on me, I always feel that no consideration whatsoever is given to our needs and feelings. Upper management (the President, Vice President of Sales, and Sales Manager) have demonstrated to me on various occasions that they have no confidence in my judgment or accomplishments, and are only interested in immediate results. They never praise or congratulate me for a fine job; they just make demands and expect them to be met. When they want me to acquire a particular new account, they pressure me, and if I should manage to open the new account, they offer no praise or show any signs of satisfaction.

I devoted two years trying to get a particular account. During that time, whenever the President or Vice President met me, he had only one question: 'What about the account?' They didn't even ask, 'How are you?'. I finally managed to establish a good relationship with the vice president of that company, leading to my getting the account.

I received a large order and established the groundwork for future business amounting to $250,000 a year. However, I received no praise — not even a handshake for this prime account. My only satisfaction came from within, because I knew I had done an excellent job and the sense of competence motivated me to carry on the good work.

What annoys me most is that management has concealed from me all information about sales, and has refused to supply me with current computerized record of my sales. They only let me know when sales are off in an account, and push me to improve it. Since I have access to the accounting records, I periodically examine my accounts, and have found that, over the course of three years, I have made substantial increases in total sales in about 90% of my accounts. I have not received proper recognition of this accomplishment.

Also, once I establish a good size account, management wants to dominate it. They make agreements behind my back by cutting prices and making themselves look good, when they should give me the privilege of telling my account that I have been able to get them a better price."

✳

The more I think of the concept of membership the more profound it seems to me. It is a concept of great heuristic value — it provides immense opportunity for further discoveries in the fields of group dynamics, sociology and anthropology. I am amazed how current literature focuses more on leadership than membership. It seems clear to me that solidarity of a group or a nation depends more on quality of membership whether that of the leaders or of the rank and file. In conclusion, assessment of sense of membership is more predictive of the fate of leadership influence than any other characteristic of the leader himself or herself. To end this chapter of the book, a phrase haunts me incessantly, *leadership devoid of membership is a disaster.*

CHAPTER FOUR

LEADING AND MANAGING

LEADER/MANAGER CONTROVERSY

Whenever the subject of leadership was approached in my classes or seminars I never failed to get two questions from someone in the audience. The first question: "Is a person born a leader?" to which I have a ready answer: "To my knowledge a person is born an infant." And that ends the discussion. But the second question raises hell: "What is the difference between a leader and a manager?" I usually reply: "you tell me." Only a minority dismiss the question as unimportant because they use the two terms interchangeably as having the same connotation. Those who insist that a leader is different from a manager fail to substantiate their claim. Some respondents stress only one difference and that is that a manager is a lower or mediocre version of a leader. My grandson, then about four years old did not care less about the kind of stupid toys we impose on our children. Like his grandfather he hates plastic. He always wanted to handle real things that adults handle. He comes to my study, opens a drawer, and takes out, say, a stapler, and asks, "What does that do?" He then tries it out. Next, he picks up the hole-puncher and poses the same question. This was followed by what fascinated him most — the tape dispenser. But what struck me most is the persistence of the same question about everything that fascinated him, namely, what something *does*, what is it *used for*. Never did the child ask what an object was in itself. From this I conclude that *action* is the issue. *Neither a leader nor a manager himself or herself is relevant. It is what a person does or is expected to do.*

That suggested change in my teaching to use verbs or verbal nouns instead of nouns. What a person does will define him or her. Soon we will find out that the range of actions is very wide indeed, but *actions* they are. Titles or labels will follow.

One final conclusion regarding the controversy of "manager versus leader," we must realize that usually the titles given to a person in charge of an organizational unit vary from one organization to another, and from a country to another. We encounter titles such as manager, chief, director, head, supervisor, and the like. The word *boss* applies to all these titles. I do not know of any organization that uses the term *leader* as an official title. It is used more as an attribute qualifying a boss — an authority figure in an institution, or in society, a person that has followers or power base. It may therefore be wise to ignore these titles and focus on what the person in charge is expected to do, and actually does, and how well he or she performs. After all, individuals we call managers, supervisors, or executives are usually in charge of people to direct, to coordinate, to command, to appraise, to develop, to discipline, to promote, or to fire, and more. I suggest the use of the term *leading* to denote specifically dealing with people, without ignoring the fact that we also deal with those who handle a variety of resources (material, financial, informational, among others). In most cases the people we lead are also engaged in leading others, though at lower levels in the authority hierarchy.

Let us therefore leave the labels *Leading* and *Following* aside, and focus on the actual activities undertaken by a boss in any situation. We'll start out with a comprehensive list of tasks that need to be accomplished under the direction of an individual overseeing the operation of a given unit in any institution. The list below is constructed of specific tasks that anyone can observe as the task is being performed — no matter what label is assigned to that person.

MANAGERIAL TASKS (List A)

1. Designing jobs and structuring daily work
2. Assigning tasks to different staff members
3. Delegating authority to perform the tasks
4. Coordinating (within one's unit and among different units)
5. Negotiating with internal units or external organizations
6. Setting objectives
7. Communicating, and implementing organizational policies
8. Creating systems and procedures
9. Detecting and resolving disputes
10. Monitoring or supervising daily work
11. Dealing with emergencies
12. Monitoring group progress
13. Initiating change
14. Monitoring progress of change
15. Designing and implementing reward systems
16. Developing subordinates
17. Self development

Five additional tasks or functions (*List B*)

1. Diagnosing and solving problems

2. Planning

3. Decision making

4. Communicating

5. Integrating

I must stress that the tasks in List B are not separate from the tasks that comprise List A. Rather, they cut across all the tasks included in the first list. For example, any of the tasks in List A requires the boss to detect irregularities, problems, or dysfunctions (diagnostic function) and to attempt to correct irregularities (problem solving). Problem solving requires ordering our activities in time, hence planning whether for the short-term or long-term. Communication within groups or between groups is also involved. Integration must be a primary function for any person in charge of a group since he or she is the only group member whose responsibility it is to maintain the cohesiveness or team spirit of the group. Integration therefore is not separate from problem solving, or decision making, or conflict resolution.

I might add that no single person can undertake all these tasks, which stresses function of delegation. Delegation in turn stresses the importance of follow-up and coordination. Furthermore no single person can be equally effective in all the tasks nor can he or she be equally motivated to perform all of them. I might add that *taking charge* is not confined to aggressive intervention in the course of events. In my capacity as a teacher, researcher, or consultant in the field of management, I do not feel obligated to explore all the items of either list. I found it sufficient to focus on the following six tasks:

1. Assigning tasks

2. Supervising and organizing work

3. Decision making

4. Communication

5. Dealing with conflict

6. Dealing with emergencies

I have no intention to report any of my research using these functions. But I want to select some of the results to arrive empirically at a definition of the role we call managing or leading. I ask the staff in a given unit, the target for a survey, to describe the behavior of the immediate boss in dealing with each of the six tasks, or functions. I present below cases showing how individual managers deal with different situations according to perception of their subordinates.

CASE STUDY: 1

Totally Ineffectual Manager

SUPERVISING AND ORGANIZING WORK	• *She is not competent to supervise.* • *The manager "covers" her job almost entirely.* • *She can't even manage her share of the work.*
DECISION MAKING	• *We haven't experienced any situation where her decision counts.* • *She's only responsible in making sure she has the best technical staff for herself, e.g., guys who do not have domestic problems.*
COMMUNICATION	• *She snaps more than talks.*
DEALING WITH CONFLICT	• *She is the main source of conflicts in the section.* • *She only adds oil to fire.* • *We avert her participation in any conflict handling.*
DEALING WITH EMERGENCIES	• *She faints after screaming and pointing fingers at anyone and everyone for bringing about emergencies.*

CASE STUDY: 2

Suffocating Behavior

SUPERVISING AND ORGANIZING WORK	• *She supervises to the last detail to the extent of suffocating me.* • *A lot of time is taken up in terms of organizing.* • *Not impressive at all.*
DECISION MAKING	• *Generally OK, but when it comes to money, she is normally indecisive or too cautious.* • *She is inconsistent in decisions yielding to pressures from inside and outside.*
COMMUNICATION	• *[She] can communicate quite well but not without being curt and insensitive to feelings of others. Sometimes she's O.K., depending on her mood.*
DEALING WITH CONFLICT	• *Tries to deny or push to other people.* • *Whatever conflict we have in our section still persists despite her actions.*
DEALING WITH EMERGENCIES	• *Panic!! [she] throws tantrums, shouts at anybody who comes in her way.* • *[In case of emergency] It's time to avoid her!!*

CASE STUDY: 3

Effective Manager

SUPERVISING AND ORGANIZING WORK	• *Very quick and efficient.*
DECISION MAKING	• *Very fast and [achieves] good solid solutions.*
COMMUNICATION	• *Friendly, though not clear at times.*
DEALING WITH CONFLICT	• *Very good, professional, tactful.*
DEALING WITH EMERGENCIES	• *Very tactful, good and professional.*

CASE STUDY: 4

Manager Controlled by Superior

SUPERVISING AND ORGANIZING WORK	• *Virtually no supervision and poor in organization.*
DECISION MAKING	• *Has no authority to make decisions — controlled by his superiors.*
COMMUNICATION	• *Poor communication, never tells you about meetings, etc. that you need to attend or things that he required you to do till the very last moment and everything is in a rush.*
DEALING WITH CONFLICT	• *Tries his best to handle conflicts, but no use as he has no authority.*
DEALING WITH EMERGENCIES	• *I suppose he is trying his best due to his constraints.*

CASE STUDY: 5

Perfectionist and Autocratic

SUPERVISING AND ORGANIZING WORK	• *Very strict supervision, picks on nitty-gritty things.* • *Very detailed, [work] must be perfect.* • *Requires immediate attention from us for tasks she wants you to carry out.* • *You must always be around when she wants to find you.*
DECISION MAKING	• *She is somewhat authoritative. This influences our recommendations.* • *Sometimes she is influenced by external pressure, but she can also stand firm on her views.*
COMMUNICATION	• *No problem. She orders us very well like a mother disciplining kids.*
DEALING WITH CONFLICT	• *Can be quite tactless at times.*
DEALING WITH EMERGENCIES	• *She is not very adept. She gets agitated very easily under pressure and stress.*

CASE STUDY: 6

Effective Management

SUPERVISING AND ORGANIZING WORK	• *Supervision is good — allows subordinates to set the pace of work. However, sometimes not very equitable in [work] distribution.* • *Certain officers are given less responsibilities due to their incompetence!* • *Delegates easily and accords appropriate authority for the fulfillment of the tasks.*
DECISION MAKING	• *He uses a consultative approach.* • *Often decisions are only taken after he has discussion with officers concerned.* • *Often not decisive, probably the inclination towards feelings for others.*
COMMUNICATION	• *Very good communication skills.* • *Explains issues well and covers topics adequately.*

Having gathered the statements offered by all subjects about individual managers, I then pooled the statements together thus showing the trend in a whole department. For the purpose of this book, I extracted from the findings only the responses pertaining to two critical situations: one showing the way managers in a given department deal with conflict, and the other about how they manage emergency situations. The reason for my selection here is that I believe that the real test of a manager's effectiveness shows more in crisis situations than in familiar or regular situations.

I take the liberty of extracting some of my comments about an organizational unit from a survey that I had conducted using the method described here.

TABLE 2: POOLED STATEMENTS

Dealing with Conflict

1. LACK OF AWARENESS	• *Shows no awareness of conflict.*
2. AVOIDANCE	• *Exposes his subordinates when criticized by his seniors.* • *Criticizes staff behind their back not admitting it when confronted by the person concerned.* • *Avoids handling conflict among subordinates.* • *Tends to agree with customers; concludes that employee was wrong before getting the facts [from subordinates].* • *Avoids confrontation with "difficult" subordinate.* • *Prefers not to notice conflict.* • *Pretends conflict does not exist.* • *Avoids conflict with his seniors.* • *Prefers not to get involved.* • *He is usually non-committal.*
3. DEFENSIVENESS	• *When confronted he becomes very defensive.* • *Appeals for cooperation.* • *Chooses to smooth over "peace at all cost" approach.* • *Maintains amicable relations with his peers at all times.* • *Is not aggressive enough; staff suffers the consequences.*
4. DELEGATION	• *Leaves it to others to resolve the conflict.* • *Pushes work to others.*
5. CAUSES OR EXACERBATES CONFLICT	• *Causes conflict always.* • *He is the main source of conflict in the unit.* • *He is the main source of conflict between our unit and other units.* • *Always creates conflict to show that he is the boss.* • *Tries to create waves.* • *Gets dragged into the conflict.* • *He makes matters worse.* • *Unable to resolve conflict when called upon to mediate.* • *Tries but to no avail since he does not have any authority.* • *Supports the wrong side, is biased.* • *Lacks sense of fairness.* • *Avoids handling conflict between subordinates.* • *Cannot handle technical conflict because he is not in the same line of work.*

6. MODES OF CONFRONTATION	• Sits down to discuss the issues only if subordinate insists. • He can be quite tactful. • He always wants to win. • Tends to behave in a professional and tactful manner. • Shows reasoning, remains clear-headed although sometimes dictator. • Tends to be stubborn, does not give in easily. • Handles work-related conflict by focusing on what could be done to solve problems. • Argues out but does not give the parties a chance to voice their views.
7. COMPROMISE	• Finds superficial solutions that do not address the real issues. • He is reluctant to get to the root of the problem. • Bargains.
8. BUREAUCRATIC SOLUTION	• Sticks to the rules.

TABLE 3: POOLED STATEMENTS

Dealing with Emergency Situations

1. PANIC REACTION	• She faints after screaming and pointing fingers at anyone and everyone for bringing about emergencies. • Temperamental. • Occasionally well, often disastrous. • Panic, throws tantrums, shouts at anybody who comes in her way. It's time to avoid her. • Impatient and stresses everyone else and hot-tempered. • Everyone tries to stay out of her path, like a chicken without its head.
2. DEPENDENCY	• Unable to stand on his own to deal with emergencies, lets others handle the situation, appeals for cooperation.
3. DENIAL	• Pretends he knows nothing, and tries to push the responsibility to his subordinate.
4. DEFENSIVENESS	• Covers up his faults, avoids dealing with emergencies.

5. SHIFTING BLAME	•	*He starts pointing fingers at his subordinates that the job was not properly done, that certain instructions were not carried out when no instructions were given.*
6. INITIAL PANIC FOLLOWED BY RECOVERY	•	*He gets excited at first but will calm down later and analyses the situation to come up with suitable solution.*
7. INFECTING OTHERS	•	*Very excited, so much so that people around him cannot think properly. Rather it would be quite a 'sin' [for him] to look relaxed and try to find a solution.*
8. PROBLEM-SOLVING BEHAVIOR	•	*He tries to stop the fire immediately — mobilizes, gets everybody into fire-fighting.*

REVIEW OF CASE STUDIES

Most managers were reported by their subordinates to become "agitated, excited, or panic-stricken." Some may even "throw tantrums." Thus, the manager's regressive behavior shows to everyone that is nearby. With regard to efficacy, some managers may recover and sit down to deal objectively with the demands of the situation. Others may not recover at all.

In many cases the excitable manager resorts to an arbitrary autocratic pattern of behavior — ordering people around in an erratic fashion. The manager holds on to his/her authority as the boss so earnestly that behavior degenerates into unreasonable demands and shouting. Feeling threatened, he or she loses control, and over-compensates by what many subordinates describe as unreasonable or irrational behavior.

Some managers who otherwise would be democratic in their style show a shift to a mature form of autocratic behavior. They become more directive, decisive and controlling. It's as if under the pressure of urgency they could no longer afford the flexibility that characterizes them under normal circumstances. They engage in fire-fighting and push subordinates to deliver.

LEADERSHIP, FELLOWSHIP AND FOLLOWER-SHIP

At the simplest level of common sense, *to lead* means to show someone the way to a destination (or the way to achieve a certain goal) at some point in future time. Time is of the essence here to indicate that we are dealing with a process with a beginning, a course, and an end. I submit that both leading and following are natural behavior tendencies that are manifested by every human in reaction to events in the environment. They occur either as transitory daily behavior, or frequently as more or less enduring habit systems. So let us explain briefly.

LEADING OR FOLLOWING AS DAILY BEHAVIOR

Leading and following occur as spontaneous modes of adaptation to social events. No social system can survive without leading and following as ingrained tendencies. I am talking here about conscious and voluntary behavior. Several times in a single day we volunteer giving directions to individuals who appear lost or confused, similarly we follow written or spoken directions. Often, following is an essential adaptive act that requires a measure of assertiveness such as when you ask someone to give you directions to a given destination, or show you how to operate an apparatus. The red traffic light *commands* us to stop, which we do, while the green light invites us to resume driving, which we welcome. We may order a loud person to stop shouting, but we may also stop the same sort of behavior in response to an order or request from another person.

LEADING AS HABITUAL BEHAVIOR

Leading or following may develop as a habitual mode of relating to other people as individuals or as a collectivity. Thus, we are able to identify an individual who is propelled to lead and another who prefers to follow. Some of those who choose to follow do that for good reasons, while others resort to following under duress or as a function of inability to perform without guidance. Leading or following as a habitual tendency is what psychologists refer to as personality trait, a propensity, a motive, a need, a drive, or inclination.

A friend of mine told me that she was waiting for the opportunity to cross a street where there was no traffic-light despite very heavy traffic. Next to her, stood an elderly man waiting for an opportunity to also cross safely. The elderly man would venture a step forward only to back up. He did that several times. Said my friend, "He looked pathetic and I felt a strong urge to help him, but I hesitated fearing that he would be embarrassed." She added: "While I was debating with myself the pros and cons, there comes a robust woman and without hesitation, she grabbed the old man's hand and at the first opportunity, dragged him to the other side of the street and went on her way without a word." My friend's failure to proceed from intention to action caused her a great deal of shame and self reproach. This incident is an example of what psychologists call *approach-avoidance* tendency — *to lead or not to lead.*

I must add that a person's presentation of self may influence people in a way that causes them to seek his guidance, or if you wish, his leadership. The person may have no intention to lead but finds himself coaxed to lead. Thus we encounter the interesting situation where potential followers *lead* a person to assume the role of *leading* them. Cause-effect circularity is obvious. I should stress that following should not be identified with passivity. The act of following may represent a wise choice under certain circumstances (the first level) or even a preferred way of being in society (the habitual level). It may also be due to preference to live with others on equal terms as a colleague or peer sharing membership in the same social setting. In the final analysis, leading and following are both social drives, necessary for survival and social cohesion. They are opposites in terms of semantics or logic, but they are not so from the existential perspective. In reality, the opposite of leading is either *misleading* or *not leading.* Leading and following inform each other, each implies the other and they are equally adaptive resources.

LEADING AS A FORMAL ROLE

In any formal organization, managers have to deal simultaneously with their superiors, subordinates, and peers. The situation includes a minimum of three parties: a superior (immediate boss), subordinate, and a peer. This is shown in the following figure.

––––––––

FIGURE: 2

Primary Managerial Constellation

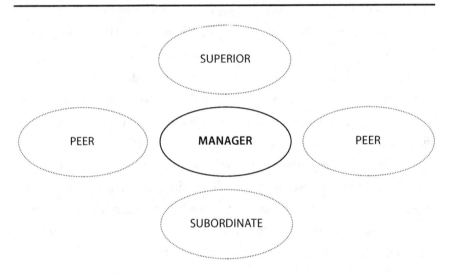

The figure does not add any information to what everybody knows. Obviously, the figure over-simplifies the situation. Only two peers and a single boss are shown in the figure for demonstration purposes. More often than not there are more peers. Furthermore, it is not uncommon that a subordinate reports simultaneously to two bosses. For example, a manager in an overseas branch of an international organization reports simultaneously to the head of the branch and to the functional head in headquarters. The figure also does not show job structure which is a potent force at the center of attention to all parties. Job requirements determine the pattern of transactions which takes place among all parties.

Meanwhile, any job requires managers to deal with their counterparts in outside organizations. There will always be regulators — internal and external, client organizations, suppliers, and many others to deal with.

Looking at this figure, the fact that hits the eyes is that there is more than leading in any leadership position. A leader at any level is simultaneously a peer (fellow) and subordinate (follower). Failure to see the three modes of behavior represents a common error of omission (or reductionism) in the leadership literature. I confess that I was guilty of the same error for decades. It was not until I presented the facts that we already knew in a visual representation that a more realistic conceptualization forced itself on my mind. I began to remind myself that there are three sets of activities in the life of any person including a person that we call leader. That is how I arrived in a previous book at the conceptualization I refer to in my teaching by the three letters, LFF, or to be more specific, LF_eF_o. The first letter refers to the function we call *leadership*. The second letter refers to *fellowship*, and the third to *follower-ship*.

LFF acknowledges a minimum of three primary roles — to actively lead, or to suspend leading for the sake of receiving (follower-ship), or take a collegiate stance (fellowship). I view the three variables as predispositions or attitudes accessible to any person, a person in leadership position included. I will define in more detail what I mean by each of the three variables starting by follower-ship, by far the feature most overlooked in characterizing leader's behavior.

FOLLOWER-SHIP (F_o)

By follower-ship, I mean readiness of an authority figure to assume a receptive posture towards another person of equal or lower rank. For example, the manager would not hesitate to solicit opinions, feedback, testing his or her views against others' views, and so on. Naturally, a person can be a passive receiver or an active receiver. In the former case, he or she submits to the will of another person. In the latter case, the manager seeks opinion, information, or advice to fulfill his or her responsibility with full awareness of accountability. Such posture fosters cooperation of the leader's group members. Cooperation gained from subordinates or peers sustains the authority of the leader. In this sense, I consider follower-ship a beneficial attitude, both rational and reality-oriented. The leader is willing to seek the counsel of some other figures who are privy to information or are otherwise more experienced and thus qualified to provide advice, counsel, or feedback. Such attitude is possible only if the authority figure is confident enough to suspend dominance in favor of consulting or seeking guidance. Curiosity, and many other cognitive assets, guide the leader's efforts in the search of clarity.

Personality traits underlying this attitude are *humility, respect for legality, and trusting the competence of the group* of which the leader is in charge. Effective use of authority requires a voluntary shift from controlling or commanding to receiving guidance. There is justification for such an approach. Often workers at the lowest level in a social system are much more in touch with the final output of the organization than middle or top management. They have the power of defeating the best of strategies.

Follower-ship is consistent with accountability. Accountability lends prudence to the leader's wielding of power. Prudence means legitimacy in wielding the prerogatives of authority. Usually, we think of accountability in relation to higher authority, but accountability should also be relative to those whom we serve. As a teacher, I am as accountable to my students as I am to those who hired me. A leader who ignores the reality of follower-ship would lack the internal controls necessary to sustain the legitimacy of his/her actions and decisions. Follower-ship may not describe the actual behavior of the leader but that of the behavior of the followers towards him or her. Such is the case when followers identify with a popular and trusted leader when they witness him in crisis or in trouble of some kind and come to his assistance.

FELLOWSHIP (F$_e$)

Fellowship is another *observable* phenomenon. Usually, a leader is surrounded by (or surrounds himself with) all types of people, some may be close personal friends. What matters here is whether the leader deals with them in a dominant fashion or in a collegiate manner as trusted staff or colleagues. I regard fellowship as a personality resource enabling an authority figure to deal with people at any rank as equal *fellow-members* of the same group or institution. In other words, the leader would focus more on the common task than asserting his or her authority. A relationship of equality enhances cooperativeness which facilitates free flow of information including authentic feedback. Competition may take place between equals but in a regulated fashion and in a spirit of fair play such as in games or debates. A leader's subordinates or peers may be candid enough to offer advice. At other times, they would not offer advice unless they are invited. Some may be included in actual policy formulation or strategy setting. Fellowship responds to the leader's need for support, which could be provided by persons whom the leader can identify with as peers, confidantes, or personal friends. Access to such people widens the leader's perspective, provides relief from the stresses of formal interactions, and reduces uncertainty. It also protects the leader from the risk of subjectivity.

Rationale of LFF Process

I view LFF as a dynamic process which consists of three distinct modes of adjustment to reality. People in leadership positions do shift back and forth between three modes of relating to others. LFF is consistent with my life experience. During my adolescent years, I was blessed by having schoolmates who served as role models to emulate. They were either colleagues of my age group or colleagues of my older brother. The latter group used to treat me as if I were of their age group when in fact I looked up to them as models. The experience of being a follower, a leader, and peer merged in my life. They alternate spontaneously. I believe my experience is consistent with the experience of many other people.

LF_eF_o Redefines Effective Leadership

When we judge a person to be a good leader, what do we really mean?
We mean that the leader in his or her capacity as a whole person has
demonstrated skill or effectiveness in utilizing resources available to him
or her. I see no sense that leading is a sovereign force in human personality,
which is severed from all other resources. Such resources are reached
through responsiveness to others' views and expertise (follower-ship), or
getting the benefit of diverse views (fellowship). A combination of
follower-ship and fellowship reflect the person's ability to forge a workable
partnership with another person or group of persons. A seasoned and self
confident leader does not limit his/her behavior to commanding. He
shifts freely (as a whole entity) from one position to another. He would be
more concerned about the outcome of his/her actions on the well-being of
an enterprise entrusted to him or her. Thus, we come to the sober
conclusion that there is more in leadership than leading behavior. In
actual practice — a leader (or let us say a boss) does not cease to be an
imperfect human person. To preserve his or her authority, he or she must
use a lot more than dominance (or better still, a lot more than his/her
ego). Fortunately, human personality has more resources than the need to
control or dominate. In the final analysis, leading is a mode of relating to
other people in more than one way. *Leadership is a relationship. It is a
process of mutual activation.* A person's *will to lead* is realized only if
someone else *chooses to follow*. Reciprocity or mutuality is intrinsic to
leadership as a social phenomenon.

Leadership role may be activated in a single act rather than in an
enduring position, such as in the case of a disaster. Studies of disaster show
the unexpected rise of leaders who undertake heroic acts that minimize
loss and save the lives of thousands of people thanks to their intervention.
Then we have the champions that volunteer more permanent activities.

The question arises: *What makes a leader who has the authority to
make unilateral decision forsake his/her legitimate power and resort to
fellowship or follower-ship?* My explanation is that he or she is mindful of
the origin of his authority, namely membership in a shared community

of people. So it seems that membership acts as a pivot around which the three LFF modes revolve. As one mode is activated, the other two recede into the background where they remain as latent resource to be activated when needed. Being rigidly stuck in one mode is dysfunctional and certainly self defeating to the leader. Let me illustrate this point by a case I came across.

> "This is the case of an executive, R&D scientist in a reputable organization. Initially, he excelled as a *developer* of his staff. He brought to the organization the best researchers in the field, and managed to form a great productive team. However, while being charismatic in the eyes of his subordinates, in the long run, he failed as a colleague of other managers in parallel units. He also failed as subordinate to higher level executives. In other words, his *leadership* eclipsed both *follower-ship* and *fellowship*. Seduced by his success, and the sense of mastery over his group, he grew blinded as to his membership and the membership of his staff in the global organization. He dealt with his staff as if they belonged exclusively to him. More seriously, he failed to see that leadership is a relationship that changes over time. Consequently, he did not see early that some — at least — of his staff outgrew their initial *loyalty* and began to aspire to participate in the organization beyond the confines of the immediate group. This case convinced me that *leadership devoid of membership spells a disaster*."

Let us ponder a little bit more the notion of leadership being a process of *mutual activation*, movement in one direction whether from a single person (a leader) to a group, or from a group to a leader ceases to be a viable relationship. Leadership is effective to the extent that it is *creative*. By that I mean that through a continued dialogue both parties gain insights which transcend their individual resources. Changes do occur as subordinates develop. Their manager would cease to exert influence if he or she fails to develop along with his subordinates. *It is the free exchange of opposing views that promises fresh insights.* Free flow of information does not occur in a culture where people are hung up on rank differential. In other words, membership must triumph over leadership. When absoluteness of power is settled in the consciousness of both the leader and the followers, the former loses his influence as an *attractive person*. Attractiveness gives way to resentment, if not hatred or contempt. Such negative feelings constitute powerful influence in reverse.

Understanding Tyranny

LFF theory sheds light on the psychology of tyranny. By tyranny, I mean arbitrary or unrestrained exercise of power. Words that enter into definition of the term *tyranny* reveal the self-defeating conduct of a tyrant: repression, oppression, abuse, or usurpation. *What do these words have in common?* They denote the leader's outright alienation and loss of legitimacy. And yet some writers refer to tyranny as a leadership *style*, albeit undesirable. That is a grave error. A tyrant's aim is not to lead, but to subjugate, suppress, vanquish, subdue, defeat, overcome, or crush. All these terms spell the end of a relationship. Power marks the end of persuasion, shared perception or dialogue. It also marks the end of shared membership. I realize that use of coercive power is sometimes necessary to maintain order and protect the system from total collapse. Functional use of coercive power implies continued identification with the social system. Furthermore, it does not violate accountability.

A tyrant, by definition, stands outside the group. His attitude towards the constituency is one of antagonism. This attitude may have developed as a result of the leader's frustrations and cumulative grievances harbored against his people. Often however, the tyrant's attitude may have been antagonistic right from the time he ascended to power. Underlying such attitude is a paranoid structure that turns the life of the leader into chronic vigilance. Subjectivity reigns supreme. Autonomy that the leader enjoys turns into autism.

MEMBERSHIP AND ORGANIZATIONAL CHANGE

The state of membership serves as a diagnostic indicator of organizational strength, especially in times of change. We must bear in mind that organizations are entities which are made up of changeable members. In robust organizations, membership change does not threaten the continued existence of the main body as an enduring institution. I say *enduring*, but not necessarily lasting forever. Dynamism of any social system is indicated by creativity in the utilization of existing members in various ways. Rotation and training policies are helpful benchmarks. Equally important in the assessment of organization endurance is the type and volume of turnover. Turnover could be a good or bad sign. It is a good sign if those who leave are replaced by more competent members. It is a bad sign if the organization is losing the best.

I know of several managers who opted to resign or take early retirement despite their desire to continue working for their respective organizations. Unfortunately, their boss was able to block subordinates' membership in the organization as a whole. Members of the team led by this manager felt like hostages deprived of their rightful membership in the global organization. In the absence of grievance procedures, subordinates find no refuge in the organization. The only way out of such misery is to quit. I found another phenomenon in conjunction with the above — the boss bypasses the immediate subordinate and directly contacts the latter's subordinates. Authority of the bypassed boss declines in the eyes of immediate subordinates and confusion spreads regarding accountability.

APPRENTICESHIP

Apprenticeship provides training in leadership through the benefits of remaining sufficiently in the role of *Follower*. Following the example of an admired boss, teacher, or coach is the way to develop future leaders who perpetuate the life of the organization. In the meantime, the apprentice acquires confidence in what he or she does, and pride in being able to identify with a master. Watching a master at work is the best means to rise to leadership position in any art. I must add that exercise of leadership role starts among peers. A healthy group composed of competent workers constitutes a fertile ground for breeding future leaders for the entire organization. In fact, as soon as a group formation is set in motion, several members emerge as potential leaders. Some group members establish presence very early in the course of group formation, others later. Still others prefer to remain in the background. Social roles emerge at different stages of group formation. A member qualifies as playing a role in the group if his or her behavior points to a pattern of intervention as a committed member in the group. The person may not be trying to establish himself as a leader in the group, but the other members of the group may end by ascribing leadership power to him or her. Pervasiveness of the team spirit facilitates the diffusion of leadership as a continuous process of influence pervading the organization at all levels. The strength of a group derives from the volume and quality of members' participation in a concerted fashion. By that I mean that each individual may compete with other individuals in contributing to the total enterprise. Cooperation shows in the readiness of each member to acknowledge the contributions offered by other members and hastens to build on other members' contributions. That produces a cumulative process of growth such as in the scientific field.

CENTRAL THESIS: MECHANISMS OF INFLUENCE

The central thesis in my theorizing is this: *Leading, Fellowship and Follower-ship* are mechanisms of influence — and influence flows both ways between people. Both those who lead and those who follow must be moving together and alternating positions along the way if they have to. One cannot just keep commanding, or dominating. Occasionally we need to walk along our charges side by side (fellowship), or even follow for the sake of progression or becoming. Furthermore, the issue is not to enable a single person to lead, but expect each member to lead without necessarily being in a leadership position. Every member is ready to provide guidance to every other member. What I am proposing is the trend of the future. With the rise of technology and expertise, management is becoming a scientific business of organizing. Hierarchical mode of management is becoming obsolete. Organizing will not be possible in a unidirectional way, neither from the top down nor from the bottom up. In fact — up and down, or top and bottom are sheer metaphors.

To end this chapter, I would like to share an incident that occurred in my life years ago. Strangely it continued to intrude in my mind as I was thinking about leadership. Going over the details of this experience, I discovered considerable relevance to many of the issues I grabbled with regarding leadership.

I will follow my free associations in recounting this story, beginning on the following page.

❋

A   J O U R N E Y   W I T H   A   D O N K E Y

Sometimes your current preoccupation brings to mind an insignificant experience that occurred decades earlier. I want to share one such experience. During WWII, my family was living at the time in Alexandria, Egypt. Alexandria became a frequent target of air raids launched by the Germans and Italians. The target was essentially the British installations and particularly the British navy vessels in the port of Alexandria. However, often the bombs hit civilian population areas. When the air raids intensified the company where my father worked decided to move its headquarters to the countryside. Naturally the whole family left but I refused to join them and stayed alone in the house. Soon afterwards the air raids worsened. So I decided to join the family.

It was not easy. First I had to take the train to Damanhur, a rural town where I boarded a second smaller local train. For the last stage of the journey there was no transportation. None that is, but a donkey which my father sent to me with a local village man. The man helped me mount the donkey. Imagine a city boy to mount a donkey. The man hit the donkey on the rear shouting, 'yalla' meaning 'go' in vernacular Arabic. Then to my surprise I saw the man heading in the opposite direction. I yelled anxiously, "Hey, aren't you going to show me the way?" "No, I have to go home," he shouted without even looking back at me. He added, "The donkey knows the way." Thus the donkey set out on *our journey.*

The man's statement, *the donkey knows the way* would appear to make no sense without knowing the mental environment in which I lived at the time. Allow me to interrupt to explain what I mean by the mental environment. I was then an undergraduate student of philosophy in Alexandria University. I had just completed a course on general psychology that taught me a lot about instinctive behavior in animals. After the initial shock of separation from the person I had hoped to be my guide, I seem to have accepted, at a cognitive level at least, the validity of the statement. I said to myself, "true, the donkey must know its way." I managed to settle for this fact, or maybe, I managed to convince myself that it was true.

Now looking back at this incident in 2010, I see clearly the dramatic change in my mental environment after years of researching the topic of leadership. This incident raises fundamental questions about leadership. I ask myself a simple question: as the donkey was moving smoothly and slowly, *Who was leading – was it me or was it the donkey?*

The first honest answer that comes to mind is, "The donkey, of course." In fact, I had surrendered completely to him — not out of passivity, but because I believed that the donkey will ultimately get me to *my* destination. That is what I thought then, as a student of psychology. But now in 2010 after 63 years, my thinking is in a different context. While I still believe that instinct is a mover of behavior and learning, I do not think the animal was capable of having a destination. He was simply repeating, almost automatically, what he has learnt from past experience. Once we arrived, I had no problem getting on foot from the donkey's endpoint to my own destination (there is a difference between an endpoint and a destination. I shall return to this subject shortly).

Allow me now to make a leap to leadership in human affairs. Leaders and their followers are supposed to share the same journey and the same destination. Leadership is a shared experience guided by shared perception of roles and objectives, but the roles are different. Let me add another equally important point — destination is not simply a location but a situation that will be reached in a future time, no matter how close. The donkey has no future. Everything in his experience is in the present time. It follows that the term destination is not applicable to an animal whose entire life is a repeat of past efforts. Naturally, this fact does not rule out certain measure of adaptability to environmental change. I do not particularly espouse a totally deterministic view of animal behavior. For animals, there is more than one path leading to an end state. This is expressed in my lectures under the title, *equifinality*. After this necessary digression allow me to resume my account of the journey.

After almost one mile, the path changed. At the first intersection the donkey, still treading slowly and deliberately, turned left. Somehow, the animal took the very edge of the path. On our right there I see a canal full of water. No sooner than the donkey settled in the new path, did he start to gallop. That lethargic, plodding creature metamorphosed into a spirited horse. I was stunned by this sudden change. Evidently what I believed was enduring lethargy concealed a great deal of *potential* or stored energy. He had more energy in store than I could fathom. Now energy reigned the animal's being, causing me a great deal of difficulty to maintain my equilibrium. What happened?

I needed to make sense of this sudden change. Could the reason be, I speculated, that the animal *felt* we are coming close to the end of his journey? The donkey must have the destination within sight, I thought. I knew from my psychology of learning experiments that a Skinner rat trained in a maze speeds up as it senses the closeness of the target at which he will be rewarded the pellet of food. This could not be the case since I knew it was too early — we had hardly made one-fifth of the distance. As I was busy trying to explain the sudden change in the animal's behavior, I glanced at the water, and there was the image of both the donkey and the rider projected unto the water ahead of us. Aha! The donkey was racing with the image projected on the water ahead of us. That realization cured me from the dismaying feeling of being subordinate to a donkey's instinct. Now the donkey is surrendering to a vision. I am once again a human, totally aware of my surroundings and have a clear idea about my destination. Then I knew the donkey could not do more than get to the end of a journey he had learnt to make by mechanical repetition.

I am not a follower after all. *But who am I then to the donkey? And what is the donkey to me?* The answer comes clearly to my mind from the role theory. I was a passenger while the animal was a vehicle of transportation, albeit a living one. I was aware of my role, while the animal was simply living his life as he had frequently done before.

The image projected into the water provided me, very early in my adulthood, with immunity against the seduction of visionary leadership. Vision that belongs to a single person is valuable to the extent that it stimulates realistic thinking about the future of a group or a person. To be of any value it has to be translated into information shared by the leader and a group. The journey from a vision to shared perception is a long one. It has to be supported by reality of the now and the anticipated future. Furthermore, there must be clear distinction between a vision and fantasy. So I never allow myself to be swept away into unthinking or unquestioning acceptance of a visionary leader.

There is something I would like to add about togetherness. I do not think there was a relationship between the donkey and me. We were, however, together in the sense of physical proximity. I was carried by the donkey and I suppose the donkey felt my body as a weight and probably as a stimulus to continue carrying me to the end. But the end was not in sight as an idea in the animal's mind. Yet for me, the end was always present as a destination and I was counting the time to reaching it.

One final point about the relationship between me as a passenger and the animal as a living means of transportation: in what way is this different from the relationship at the human level between leader and follower? First, there is no shared perception. The animal of course has sensory experience of my weight besides constant sensory input from the environment along the path the animal was treading. I add that the animal learnt behavior was not exact repetition of his past learning. This was evidenced by his ability to respond adaptively to whatever obstacle came in his path; for example he would avoid stones, get around holes in the ground, and the like. There was no togetherness in terms of sharing perception, or communication.

Within a journey of a few hours, my thinking developed from being guided by prejudice, to that of a reflective and objective human being. My first definition of the role of the animal was a transportation vehicle. The more I watched objectively regarding the change of the animal's behavior in the face of obstacles, the more I thought of him as less mechanical. His behavior changed according to the change in the quality of the path he was treading. His behavior was not totally mechanical. I began to think about instinct versus rational reflection... initially, I took it for granted that my human reasoning meant superior adjustment in all circumstances. I was humbled by the realization that instinct must, after all, be superior when it comes to sheer survival. I must also add that during this journey, learning was going on spontaneously — I developed the skill of harmonizing between myself, the rider, and the donkey.

Throughout the journey, the donkey and I were totally alone in vast fields that extended for miles around us. We never met a human soul throughout the journey. Stillness broken occasionally by muffled cacophony of sounds of barking coming from different directions at a distance adding to the mystery of the moment. Being alone in the heart of nature inevitably triggered the thought that we both share something crucial — we both inhabit the same world. It is into this world that we were thrown and from which we will depart. We both were children of nature. Nature asserted its presence in my mind.

CHAPTER FIVE

SOCIAL STRUCTURES

THE HUMAN PERSON AS A UNIVERSE

I view each individual as a *universe*, a highly complex bio-psycho-social system as we stated earlier. In view of its complexity, it would be naive to just approach the other individual in a random fashion. We need a framework, or a map, to delimit the area we intend to explore in this vast universe that we call individual. Scientists would call such framework *model* simply because it constitutes a standard guide in our attempt to explore a complex terrain. The model helps us focus on certain aspects of personality of any person. Meanwhile it is applicable to a person's attempt to describe him/or herself as well. Another way to explain what is meant by a descriptive model is a map of the road, the boundary of the terrain you need to explore or want to apprehend. It does not really matter which model we choose as long as we are clear that the model is a perspective from which we gain access to what we are interested to know about oneself or another. The model may also be revised and expanded to accommodate our growing awareness.

The model I recommend is the oldest in the modern history of scientific psychology. However, it had its roots in ancient philosophy since the time of Greek philosophers. I use it because of its simplicity. It *guides* rather than *replaces* common sense. Naturally, a psychologist must go beyond and use scientifically designed instruments. In daily encounters, it would make sense to meet people at the same level of common sense. As Karl Jaspers asserts, "the truth begins when two people meet." The most important rule in daily encounters is the need to know. And to *know* demands a dialogue which is enhanced by *authenticity*. Let us then go to the model. The model draws our attention to three modes of mental (or psychological) activity. By *mode* I mean a global state of mind:

1. Cognitive Mode
2. Affective Mode
3. Conative Mode

I present below brief definitions of the three modes. I will use 'CAC,' the first letters of the modes for future reference to the model.

1. *The Cognitive Mode — Knowing*

The cognitive mode is a state of thinking about the world for the sake of understanding and satisfying the inquisitive mind. In this mode, all sorts of mental processes are activated ranging from sensory perception to reasoning through memorizing, recalling, or imagining. When we are in this mode, we may be described by an outside observer as being *primarily* pensive or reflective. In other words, our contact with reality is primarily at an intellectual level.

2. *The Affective Mode — Feeling*

The affective mode refers to a person who displays some affect (feeling or emotional reaction) to a perceived occurrence in the environment or in one's body or mind. The feeling tone could be pleasant such as joy, warmth, sentimentality, excitement or enthusiasm. Or it could be unpleasant such as anger, jealousy, suspicion, anxiety, guilt or shame. The affective mode may be mild or intense, superficial or deep. The affective mode is said to be deep when it reverberates at different regions of the psyche.

3. The Conative Mode — Striving[18]

Conatus is the Latin term for exertion. It is defined as the force in every animate creature toward the preservation of its existence. More specifically, it is the natural tendency to act, to reach out for a goal. The *conative* mode could be mere impulse, or craving, or desire. The whole body would be aroused. It could also be manifest striving for goal attainment. Successful progress towards the goal is always accompanied by experience of pleasure, and goal attainment is accompanied by sense of pleasure. In contrast, continued obstruction of striving is always accompanied by feeling of frustration.

The concept of conation is a reminder of Bergson's[19] *élan vital*, or *vital impulse*. Bergson suggests that there is an original "impetus of life," life being defined as "a tendency to act on inert matter." The concept of conation implies that every living entity is goal directed, in contrast with a mechanistic theory of living organisms.

Conation seems to have its roots in nature. It brings to mind the phenomenon of *tropism* (Greek *tropē*, or a turning). This is the tendency of say a plant, to respond to a particular natural stimulus such as light *(phototropism)*, or heat *(thermo tropism)*, or gravity *(geo tropism)*, or water *(hydro tropism)*. The response to chemical stimuli is called *chemotropism*. There are as many of such phenomena as there are natural

---

[18] The term conation is no longer widely known. I am grateful to Lee Lee Yong for drawing my attention to the fact that it was listed by Wikipaedia in "The 1,000 most obscure words in the English language."

[19] Bergson, H. (1998). *The Creative Evolution* (transl. A. Mitchell). Mineola, New York: Dover Publications (first published 1911).

sources of stimulation. A movement toward the source of stimulation is known as positive *tropism*, whereas a movement away from the source is called *negative tropism*.

Tropism exists also in living creatures. An individual organism may exhibit a positive or negative tropism to the same stimulus at different times, depending on the strength of the stimulation and the internal physiological condition of the organism. Among the animals, conation is a mere impulse or instinctive striving. Edward MacNeal (2003)[20] noted "that even at birth, a calf has inborn cognition that will drive it to struggle quickly to its feet [conation] no matter what, and will then impel it to run if a lion charges. There hasn't been time for the calf to learn to run; it may have never seen any creature run, yet it will run." Christine Janis and Peter J. Darman wrote that "wild beasts have evolved the ability to get to their feet and start moving remarkably soon after birth; some can run at near adult speed within half an hour after birth and can keep up with the herd within a day."[21]

Going back to the three modes, McDougall (1933)[22] pointed out that they should not be viewed as *three phases* of mental activity. Rather, they should be seen as "three distinguishable and inseparable aspects of *one complex activity*; for they occur in intimate interplay with one another." McDougall gives the example of a baby in the crib wanting to be carried by the mother, the whole body moves upward towards the mother. Here, *striving* is prominent, but it occurred in association with seeing the mother and recognizing her (cognition). Meanwhile there is an element of excitement which is likely to give rise to pleasant feeling. In contrast, if the mother does not respond, the thwarting of the striving is accompanied with feeling of unpleasantness. McDougall warns that we should not properly speak of the three modes as *faculties*, if by 'faculties' we mean powers that can be independently exercised. He adds that the

---

[20] MacNeal, E. (2003, Summer). *Etc: A Review of General Semantics*, pp. 124–137.
[21] Quoted by MacNeal (2003).
[22] McDougall, W. (1933). *The Energies of Men: A Study of the Fundamentals of Dynamic Psychology*. New York: Charles Scribner's Sons.

three modes of mental functioning seem to be *ultimate*. By ultimate, McDougall means that *none* of them could be analyzed into constituents that are still simpler or more elementary functions.[23]

It should be stressed, however, that despite the fact that these three modes are inseparable, they characterize every phase of mental activity. Meanwhile, they vary greatly in intensity or prominence from moment to moment. As McDougall observes:

> "When we are making a strong effort, whether bodily or mental, the striving aspect [conation] is intense and prominent in our consciousness. When we attain, or come close to the goal towards which we strive, pleasant feeling is prominent. When our striving is checked and thwarted, the whole activity is unpleasant. When we are engaged with some familiar mildly interesting matter, as when we read a novel, chat with a friend or listen critically to familiar but not very good music, the cognitive aspect is most prominent."[24]

Let me offer a few examples to further clarify McDougall's assertion. When we judge a person to be *reserved and cool*, what we really mean is that *cognition* tends to dominate this person's affect or feelings. We do not imply that the person has no feelings, but that his feelings are subdued, or under tight control. Our judgment is confirmed by the fact that he impresses other people as being cold or unsympathetic. Meanwhile, we will note that this person tends to be at the same time deliberate in taking action — he or she would tend to delay action, to *think* before acting.

Let us take another example of a person in a state of tension. He appears restless, fidgety and driven *(conative)*. Simultaneously, he would be feeling anxious and worried. Naturally, negative feelings and disturbed urges will inevitably interfere with the individual's cognitive functioning. Meanwhile, he would not be able to cope with demands of reality *(conation)*. Thus a vicious circle is set in motion where disturbance in one

---

[23, 24] See at left: McDougall, W. *The Energies of Men*, pp. 147–148.

element of the CAC triad exacerbates disturbance in the other two. The fact that the three facets are contiguous has practical implications. Intervention to help a person under stress may start anywhere. Thus we may adopt a *rational* approach, which favors a cognitive thrust. We help the subject understand his or her condition with the hope that he would gain mental control of the situation. Or we may initially provide sympathetic support followed by a cognitive approach. A third alternative strategy is encouraging the individual to take one or the other courses of action to remove sources of stress.

✳

I started out by saying that the three modes are helpful in understanding individuals, your *self* included. I did not mean understanding the overall character or personality of an individual. I meant understanding the condition at a given moment in time. We must distinguish between two notions, *personality traits* and *mood states*. The former refers to enduring characteristics which we could only detect had we had the chance to observe the individual in a variety of life situations. A *mood state* is a transitory emotional condition. Mood fluctuations are inevitable even in the healthiest of individuals. Witnessing a person in a depressed mood does not justify jumping to the conclusion that pessimism is typical of that individual's personality or character make-up. A person characterized by an optimistic outlook on life may experience a depressed mood in reaction to a serious crisis. People around this person would note that he is not *being himself*. However, we should guard against a common belief that being a passing state, a mood is less significant than a personality trait. In fact, there are situations where a passing mood may endanger a person's life. Take for example driving a car in heavy traffic while being absent-minded or preoccupied with all sorts of worries. Or take the example of a person facing a critical examination or employment interview while in a similar mood. A euphoric mood may be just as hazardous. It tends to conceal signals of impending danger. Such failure in cognition may lead to disastrous decisions.

So far the center of our attention has been the mental states of the individual *in general*. But we all know that an individual *in general* does not exist. Only specific individuals exist and they exist *in relation* to the world in which they live. We encounter them as members in various social structures — dyadic, triadic, small groups, or large groups of varying size and complexity such as tribes, corporations, or nations. Furthermore, the individuals within any of these social structures encounter different situations which demand different modes of participation. It is not difficult to note that different aspects of the individual's personality are revealed in different social structures and in different situations within each (see Appendix for different levels of social structures). In the next section we will talk about *dyadic* and *triadic* structures. It is not the author's intention to offer a textbook type of account. The author's intent is to counteract a common tendency of seeing phenomena out of context. In the remaining section of this part of the book, we will follow the individual as a participant in various social structures starting with *dyadic* and *triadic* structures.

DYADIC STRUCTURES

A dyad is a social unit of two individuals. A single individual may be a member in multiple dyads each of which responds to different needs, satisfies different life goals, and activates different functions. The conditions under which dyads are formed vary considerably. A dyad may be formed after brief encounters during which some kind of affinity, or interest, draws the parties to each other. Other dyads may develop gradually after several encounters. Some dyads are short-lived while others last for a lifetime. It is important to note that dyadic formations are ubiquitous and necessary for the sustenance of social systems of a larger number of people. The reader may have already imagined a mother with a newborn baby, an eternal dyad in which the mother and the baby are instinctively drawn to each other. Both are biologically prepared, and culturally conditioned for the bond. While the dyad is embedded in the social system, it stands out as a prominent figure against the social landscape as a backdrop or context.

FIGURE: 3

Dyadic Encounter

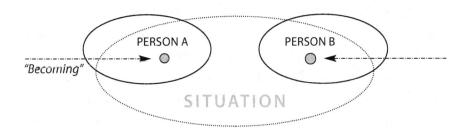

There are many other culturally-determined dyads, such as the following: husband–wife, coach–apprentice, doctor–patient, teacher–student, boss–subordinate, chief–deputy and maybe many others. There are roles certain individuals habitually assume in relating to others in more or less enduring dyadic formations: disciple, confidante, confessor, guardian, lover or mistress, and *nemesis*, namely, a habitual rival. There are also certain jobs which require dyadic teams; for example, doctor–nurse, police officer–crime investigator.

ANALYSIS OF DYADIC STRUCTURES

It is easy to understand a dyad where a measure of harmony is required and can be reached if the roles are clearly defined in terms of the parameters referred to earlier, namely responsibility, authority and accountability. Still differences are inevitable, but one would hope that they could easily be ironed out given a culture with clear job definitions, objectives, rules and regulations, which could settle conflicts in essentially rational *(or cognitive)* manner and according to well-established legalities.

I am of course oversimplifying here, to stress that a dyad embedded in a formal and well managed system does not face the challenges of maintaining harmony that a personally formed dyad will be faced with. However, rationality of a large formal system does not remove the reality of the normal structure of human personality. Here we must appeal to the three modes referred to in the CAC model. Rational members of a dyad will react emotionally to certain situations and experience frustration in their striving to meet the expectations of the other party. There will always be obstacles delaying or impeding their striving to attain expected or desired goals. How the members of the dyad will face such obstacles will depend on the degree of harmony they have been able to establish. Perfect harmony is impossible in human relationships. There will always be differences — *cognitive, affective, and conative.* The issue is not wiping out differences, but anticipate and recognize them when they occur, better still, before they occur. Shared perception of the issues over which the parties differ is crucial. If the members engage in a dialogue about the issues, chances are they may be able to resolve the conflict at their level. In a formal system, the conflicting parties are not left alone. The system may come to their rescue. Even if problems persist, the repercussions on members of a dyad are not disastrous. This is because they are partially included and the relationship is essentially formal.

The situation is completely different if the dyad is personal, such as in friendship; still more difficult in a dyad which is supposed to last for a long time, such as in marriage. The author cannot turn this chapter to a counseling forum. He can only share a number of scientific facts for the reader to start out with.

1. *Acceptance of Otherness*

You must accept the *otherness* of your partner as a fact of life: No matter how well you think you know the partner, there is still so much you do not know and will not know on your own. Furthermore, the other person may not know everything about himself or herself. The issue is not knowledge, rather it is *understanding.* We need to share the knowledge which helps sustain the dyad. It is clarity that we need. In fact, too much knowledge about the other person is not needed and may even harm the relationship. It is more serious if you probe too much. The relationship is harmed if the person discovers you are privy to private information. No matter how much you love the other person, his or her privacy should not be violated.

2.   *The Issue of Self Definition*

It is easy to start a relationship, but sustaining it over time is the issue. A lot of learning takes place in the course of a dyad's life. But the members must have the desire to learn. Individuals enter into an association with *assumptions* about the *nature* of the partner. At sometime in the history of the relationship one or the other of the pair will experience a shock when the partner violates the assumption. The shock is displayed by a common statement such as: "You are a husband or father, you are supposed to..." Rarely do partners share definition of the roles in the relationship. Each holds his own definition. We discover late in the relationship that the other party behaves in the relationship in the light of his definition of the role. Role definition is usually determined by the way the person defines himself — not only in the current relationship — but also elsewhere. The problem is compounded by the fact that an individual may not be clear about his or her own self definition. He or she discovers it as he goes along in life. In fact a relationship may be a means to discover the way we define ourselves in any relationship.

3.   *The Issue of Intimacy*

On the whole, one or the other member of a dyad may manifest anxiety when the partner is seen to be coming too strongly or too close. Alternatively, he or she may feel that the other is occasionally remote or indecipherable. So a high degree of sensitivity is required in the way we approach another individual. This brings to mind the fable of the two porcupines:

"One wintry day a couple of chilled porcupines huddled together for warmth. They found that they picked each other with their quills; they moved apart and were again cold. After much experimentation, the porcupines found the distance at which they gave each other some warmth without too much sting."[25]

The fable raises the issue of comfort in intimacy: how close can we get without interfering with each other? How much warmth we need and how much we can give to the other? Harmony in a relationship requires a measure of sensitivity to the partner's tolerance of, or need for warmth.

An element of harmony is required for the sustenance of the association. I say, *a measure of harmony*, because perfect harmony is impossible due to inevitability of differences. We often meet a dyad consisting of parties who are different, but complementary. We may meet others who are similar, but in conflict with each other, occasionally or frequently. However, they continue to guard the bond for either of two reasons, one is that they were able to face the conflict and cope with it. The other reason is they would rather live with the conflict than face the unknown if they break up. That is how many relationships persevere despite agonizing contradictions.

4.   *The Issue of Open Boundary*

No matter how intimate the relationship is between the pair of a dyad, the dyad is embedded in a social system. It is affected by its surroundings. It may also exert influence on its surroundings. We must also remember that each member of a dyad necessarily holds membership in several other dyads, triads, groups and other larger social systems. However, there are dyads that develop apart from society. Such is the case with illicit love affairs, or delinquent associations. However, the individual members still continue to maintain their relationships in their primary groups. It is the association that they try to keep secret.

---

[25] Bellak, L. (1970). *The Porcupine Dilemma: Reflections on the Human Condition.* New York: Citadel Press.

VALUE OF DYADIC FORMATION

Members of a dyad serve as occasion for both to make discoveries about themselves. Each may serve as a mirror reflecting back characteristics unknown to him or her. They provide support to each other. They can do together what they are unable to do alone. Shared activities may be beneficial or harmful to the system they function within. The important thing to know is the dyad is a social unit which performs functions neither of the members can perform alone.

DYADIC STRUCTURES AND LEADERSHIP

Leading a nation or any large social system is an awesome affair. There are moments when the leader experiences loneliness at the top. No human individual has the capacity to fulfill the function alone. He or she needs a coterie of trusted associates to contribute their different skills and wisdom to the person in charge. But the formal assistance the leader gets will not be enough. This because the leader is at the same time a *human* person who needs support in his capacity as human, not just a public figure. That is how history teaches us that leaders in high places have always availed themselves of intimate dyadic opportunities. Besides the formal advisors, the leader needs close associates, preferably outside the formal system, with whom the leader dispenses with his or her public persona and gets the benefit of intimacy. History instructs us that many great leaders had availed themselves with this privilege.

Examples of famous dyads: President Kennedy and his brother Bob, Nasser and Amer, or Nasser and Hussein Heikel in Egypt, Chairman Mao and Chou En-lai in China. These dyads we know of because they have been revealed by historical accounts. However, the reader can identify similar examples in organizations.

TRIADIC STRUCTURES

In the previous section, we talked about the dyadic structures and their dynamics. Mere addition of a third member turns a dyad to a much more complex social unit. I would like to stress at the outset an important fact. The difference between a dyad and a triad is much more qualitative than quantitative. The qualitative difference is evidenced in the fertility of the dyadic structure in terms of the number of social roles that are likely to emerge. One or more of the following roles may occur:

1. *Mediation:* When a dispute occurs between two members, an opportunity presents itself to the third person to intervene as arbiter or mediator.

2. *Conspiracy:* Two members may conspire, or team up, against the third.

3. *Jealousy:* Two members may turn into rivals competing for the love of the third.

4. *Leadership:* The opportunity for leadership presents itself to any of the three members. Alternatively any pair has the opportunity to assign the leading role to the third member.

The four events cited above are matters of probability. But let us have a look on what actually happens in reality. Soon we will note that there are many tasks which require a team consisting of three interdependent roles. Examples I could think of are:

1. *In the legal sphere:* plaintiff, defendant, and judge

2. *In court of law:* prosecutor, defense lawyer and judge

3. *In flying a military plane:* pilot, navigator and gunner

4. *In negotiation:* two contestants and mediator, or arbitrator

5. *In the medical field:* doctor, nurse, and assistant nurse (or attendant)

THE NATURAL TRIAD

Researchers in social psychology and anthropology found out the prevalence of a conflict resolution system in traditional cultures. The system involves three participants. It is referred to in literature as the *Natural Triad.*[26]

FIGURE: 4

The Natural Triad

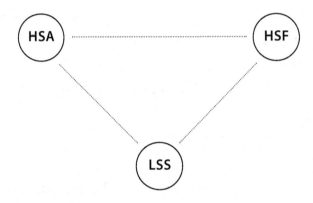

The three participants in the Natural Triad include:

a.   High-status Authority (HSA)

b.   High-status Friend (HSF)

c.   Low-status Subordinate (LSS)

Let me explain how this system works. In traditional cultures, tension builds up frequently between an authoritarian father (HSA) and son (LSS). Another authority figure (HSF), usually an uncle, intervenes in favor of the son. Interestingly, as researchers found out, the uncle could be either the maternal or the paternal uncle, depending on whether the kinship

---

[26] Freilich, M. (1964, August). The natural triad in kinship and complex systems. *American Sociological Review*, vol. 29, no. 4.

system of the family is patriarchal or matriarchal. The *Natural Triad* seems to have the benign effect of restoring harmony where it occurs.

A closer look at the figure below will show that the triad is made up of three interdependent dyads:

a.   HSA & LSS

b.   HSF & LSS

c.   HSA & HSF

FIGURE: 5

Interdependent Dyads of the Natural Triad

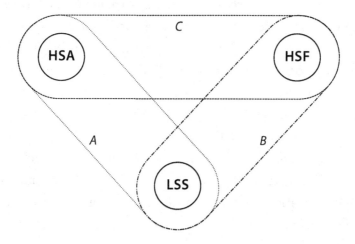

This means that dyads are embedded as constituents of triads. Meanwhile, we should not forget that the system is a process which is set in motion when harmony of the social system is disrupted by injustice. Three roles are activated to restore the harmony. The lesson that we learn here is that the triad is not a frozen entity. Rather it is a process of exchange involving three individuals, each of whom has a role to play in a tradition that helped the survival of the global system.

I appreciate the efforts of anthropologists and social psychologists who identified the natural triad in preliterate cultures. Their discovery enables us to identify similar phenomena in modern formal organizations and in large families, even though they occur sporadically and randomly. It often happens that an employee who suffers injustice perpetrated by an unjust authoritarian boss appeals to a former boss, a mentor. The subordinate avails himself of this habitual mentor. The mentor may or may not approach the boss in an effort to resolve the conflict. More often than not, the mentor does not go beyond offering emotional support to the unhappy subordinate. This is an informal version of the natural triad, which could be implemented as a formal procedure.

In fact the same phenomenon occurs frequently in many families, though with a cast different from that observed in the *Natural Dyad*. For example, a married couple who suffers frequent bouts of conflict, somehow manages to involve a third person who takes up the role of mediator. I would like to add that involving a third party may be a *political* move taken by one member to alter the power structure in his or her favor. Be it as it may, the involvement of a third party implies that a dyad has to *evolve* to a triad which is a social arrangement that enhances the probability of conflict resolution.

We often find a triadic formation involving two subordinates and their boss. Unable to handle a difficult subordinate the boss initiates the process of mediation. He calls on a trusted subordinate to straighten out the difficult subordinate. Here we have the phenomenon of *natural triad in reverse,* as shown in Figure 6.

In this triad the boss delegates the role of mediation to his trusted subordinate. So instead of having two formal authority figures negotiating the terms for resolution of conflict, we get in this example a formal authority figure activates an influential subordinate to perform the mediation function. This phenomenon is observed in large families where one son is *authorized* by the father to handle a difficult son. Here is a situation where personal influence can be put to avoid the negative repercussions of the use of coercive power of formal authority.

FIGURE: 6

Natural Triad in Reverse

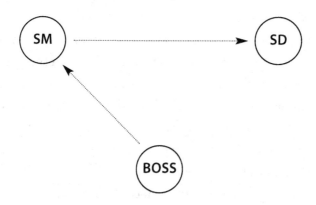

Represented in the figure above: SM = mediating subordinate;
SD = other subordinate; Boss (HSA, high-status authority).

Levels of Social Structuring
It is important to remember that the triads emerge in a larger system that
includes several dyads and triads. That brings us to the next level of social
structuring, namely the *small group.*

S M A L L   G R O U P

Definition of Small Group
In the previous two sections, we followed individuals as they interact
within dyadic and triadic social structures. In this section, we shed some
light about the behavior of individuals as they gather in a third social
structure, namely a small group. *The first question we must ask is what
constitutes a small group?* Most social psychologists define a small group
as a group that has three or more individual members. The maximum size
is implicit in the alternative label, *face-to-face* group. In other words, a

group is small if its constituent members are able to interact directly. Face-to-face interaction is a convenient criterion of the smallness of a group. We are free to determine the size of the group as long as the space where members meet allows convenient face-to-face interaction. They are then able to communicate directly and instantly with one another.

However, I object to *three* being the lower limit of the size of a small group. The reason is that a group of three, a *triad*, as demonstrated above, proved to be a universal social structure that can stand on its own as a distinct social entity. Focusing on the triad as a distinct social entity reveals significant human phenomena that are likely to remain hidden if a triad is diluted in a larger social entity.

Going back to the condition of face-to-face interaction as defining criterion for the smallness of a group, we must bear in mind that members of the same groups may work apart from each other. However, the criterion of interface still holds, since the workers must meet regularly from time to time for reasons of coordination, planning, problem-solving, or resolving conflicts. Meanwhile groups composed of geographically dispersed members are becoming more common, and, consequently, they use computer-mediated forms of communication. It may very well be that the quality of face-to-face interaction would decline as a result of dispersion.

A fundamental axiom of social psychology is that the group is more than the *sum total* of its members. I repeated this axiom hundreds of times until I came across the following statement made by Koffka, (1935):[27]

> "It has been said: the whole is more than the sum of its parts. It is more correct to say that *the whole is something else than the sum of its parts*, because summing is a meaningless procedure, whereas the whole-part relationship is meaningful." [my emphasis]

---

[27] Koffka, K. (1935). *Principles of Gestalt Psychology*. New York: Harcourt, Brace & Company, p. 176.

It was only then that I stopped to think of the serious implications of the concept of *summation* of parts. Summation is a quantitative property that does not describe a group as a social entity. A group is *qualitatively* different than a sheer assemblage of individuals. A group develops as a result of interaction. In other words, a group is an *emergent* entity which develops along with the process of the exchange that will take place among participants. Koffka's observation is consistent with a statement made by John Dewey (1954)[28], which I frequently quote in teaching. John Dewey states:

> "The actions and passions of individual men are in the concrete what they are, their beliefs and purposes included, because of the social medium in which they live; that they are influenced throughout by contemporary and transmitted culture, whether in conformity or protest. What is generic and the same everywhere is at best the organic structure of man, his biological make-up. While it is evidently important to take this into account, it is also evident that none of the *distinctive* features of human association can be deduced from it." p. 195

The key point in Dewey's statement is that *none of the distinctive* features of a group can be deduced from our prior knowledge of individual members of the group. It follows that the notion of *summation* is not only *meaningless* as Koffka has noted, but it is also misleading. What the members contribute must be *relevant* to the reason for which the group came into existence. Relevance to an external purpose implies that individuals join the group with the intent to participate in a more or less unpredictable enterprise. Group life is a social occasion for individuals to exert influence on each other in the light of their understanding, and acceptance, of the mission of the group. The outcome could not be properly described as a result of summation of individual contributions,

---

[28] Dewey, J. (1954). *The Public and Its Problems*. Chicago: Swallow Press, p. 195.

such as contribution of money to a collection box. A more apt analogy would be the process of chemical interaction. Mixing oxygen with hydrogen initiates a process of chemical interaction producing water, a third substance *other* than the original substances. As people interact and influence one another, the group materializes as a social field whose dynamics will transcend individuals' contributions.

A group is a more complex social entity than either a dyadic or triadic social structure. Increased complexity is a double-edged property. On one hand, it mobilizes diverse resources, mental and otherwise. Meanwhile, members are given the opportunity to play different social roles in the pursuit of collective objectives. On the other hand, complexity gives rise to more contradictions and dilemmas that the group may not be able to reconcile. However, coping with challenges and dilemmas is the very essence of the process which engages group members in their efforts to reach consensus.

Describing a Group

We make a big mistake if we describe a group in the same way we describe a continuous person with definite height, size, color, weight and enduring personality characteristics. The group has definite beginning, but neither its course nor its end is predictable. With regard to the end, a group may have a *stated* objective, but the objective is not the end. Rather, it is an idea in the mind of an agent or agency which had assembled people with the hope to attain that stated end. This amounts to saying that a group *becomes* a group only when individuals have accepted to engage in a collective action. Otherwise the group is a process of becoming. The process is perpetuated by members who play different roles. The roles are bound to be different because of the diversity of character make-up of the participants, their life experiences. The issue of *diversity versus homogeneity* is a factor that should be considered in relation to the mission of the group. The will to participate is an equally important factor to consider — it determines the degree to which diversity will be deployed and made use of. The will to participate implies opening the boundary of *self* to send, and receive, messages. A note of caution is in order here: It would be wrong to think that the superiority of the group over simpler structures is absolute. Its superiority depends on the utilization of its unique advantage which derives primarily from the optimum deployment of diversity. *Failure to manage diversity spells chaos.*

One of the main purposes of this section of the book is to draw attention to the group as a *dynamic process* rather than a *static* entity. Social psychologists have been much more interested in studying intergroup relations while shying away from the study of internal dynamics. My claim is supported by a comprehensive review of the literature, heroically undertaken by Wittenbaum and Moreland (2008).[29] They concluded:

> "The field of social psychology is filled with research on attitude change, prejudice, self-concept formation, stereotyping, and emotions, most of which has ignored how these processes operate in small groups. This neglect means that many questions central to the human social experience have not been investigated. As the field of social psychology advances, it will become increasingly important to consider the operation of people's thoughts and feelings in more complex and dynamic social situations." p. 188

SMALL GROUPS AND THE GLOBAL ORGANIZATION

A small work group is the basic unit of the corporation as much as a nuclear family is the basic unit of the extended family or the tribe. I must stress at this point that individuals become members of the corporation via small groups. Small groups are formed at different levels of the authority hierarchy. Individuals pass through many groups and at different authority levels in the course of a single employment. I might

---

[29] Wittenbaum, G. M. & Moreland, R. L. (2008). Small-group research in social psychology: Topics and trends over time. *Social and Personality Psychology Compass 2/1*, pp. 187–203.

add that strategic decisions, policy formulation, and structural changes take place in small groups at the highest level of organizations. Furthermore, top management in business or government consists of small groups. In addition, *informal* groups, called sometimes *primary groups*, develop spontaneously within organizations, and at different levels of the authority hierarchy. We all know about clubs and cliques of executives who share common interests.

Experts in social psychology of industry claim that informal structure of organizations is as real as formal structure. Brown[30] (1954) stressed the function of the primary groups in the socialization of individuals in society. He states:

> "The primary group is the instrument of society through which in large measure the individual acquires his attitudes, opinions, goals, and ideals; it is also one of the fundamental sources of discipline and social controls. Although some of the individual's attitude and ideals are acquired actually within the primary group, others come from his culture or sub-cultures. To a considerable extent, however, it is through the primary group (and especially the family) that these are enforced and handed on. It is the social pressure of the primary group which, in most people, becomes the instrument of discipline and moral control. It is also the source of other controls which are not moral controls in the strict sense of the work, such as those based on a code of behavior suited to the circumstances in which the group was placed."

Note that Brown was writing about primary groups at such an early time (1954) without realizing that most of such groups were small according to the interface criterion. Evidently face-to-face interaction in small groups has always been, and I suppose, will continue to be the most powerful and ubiquitous mechanism of socialization. I must also add that socialization

---

[30] Brown, J. A. C. (1972). *The Social Psychology of Industry*. Middlesex, UK: Penguin Books (first published 1954).

in small groups never stops. It starts in the family, but continues in various small groups beyond the boundary of the family sphere. Sadly and surprisingly, this feature is overlooked in personality theory and in social psychology research.

Transitory Teams

One of the most striking features of change in the current business environment is the increasing reliance of management on temporary teams which are formed for the purpose of attaining definite objectives after which the teams disband. Members of these teams come from different disciplines in the same firm or from altogether different firms. Quite often, participants in these teams are strangers to each other and have no legitimate authority over one another. Thus, they rely exclusively on their personal resources in their attempts to exert influence on one another. Organizations' increased dependency on temporary teams implies recognition on behalf of management of these organizations first, that current formal structures cannot adequately cope with the increasing complexity of business problems. Therefore, the solution of those problems requires the mobilization of groups of specialists from diverse disciplines. Second, that due to the unpredictability of the market, task forces must be quickly assembled to deal with unexpected events. Evidently, work in such transitory and discontinuous settings presents serious challenge to managers who are used to settle in the same positions for a relatively long time, supervising the same constituency, and dealing most of the time with regular and *'expected'* problems. Precedence and past experience, combined with goodwill, could help them.

Regular Meetings

Another phenomenon that needs much attention is the almost compulsive reliance on meetings. According to *Fortune* magazine, the typical American manager spends 30% to 70% of the day in meetings. In many meetings, 20% of the people do 80% of the talking.[31] I am grateful

---

[31] *Fortune* magazine, March 23, 1992.

to *Fortune* magazine to have provided statistical confirmation of my own observations in several organizations around the world. Often, you will witness managers rushing from one meeting to the other leaving unfinished important projects. Just imagine yourself a manger, leaving unfinished an important task to rush to a meeting, albeit important, but mentally unprepared. You participate to the best of your ability — tolerating controversies, ambiguities, occasionally looking at your watch thinking about the next meeting. Towards the end of the meeting, that is if you were lucky enough to know that the meeting will soon end, concerns about the next meeting intrudes into your mind. Physically, you are still in the current meeting, but mentally you are somewhere else. As soon as the meeting ends, you rush hoping to arrive promptly at the next meeting. If you are fortunate, the meeting would be held in the same building. Often it requires driving to another location. You arrive safely and sit there trying to contain yourself, and establish presence in a novel situation with different types of people.

It seems to me that the problem here is not just the frequency of meetings, but the dovetailing of meetings, poor timing — holding meetings close to the end of the day when people are getting ready to go home. In the US and some European cities, commuting between work and home is in itself an ordeal. Often, meetings have the effect of torture. They go on for hours without breaks. I learnt a lot about the futility of some meetings from comments I heard from participants. More revealing were the doodles that participants leave behind. Before ending this section about small groups, I will share some thoughts about the art of running meetings. But let me say something about group solidarity.

Team Spirit and Its Dangers

Managers may push for maximum solidarity, cohesiveness, and harmony as supreme values that should characterize the groups they manage. You often hear words such as *bonding, team spirit, and team player* as values in the absolute sense. Often these terms end by becoming more slogans rather than principles. A member in the opposition may be denied the honor of being a *team player*. In reality *that member may be the very person whom the team needs to get out of an impasse*. While being unrealistic, driving for maximum solidarity may ultimately lead to conformity. *Conformity, by definition, defeats the very purpose of a group.* As we pointed out earlier, the unique advantage of a group is that it is a setting where individual contributions flow into public consciousness. Opposing views and different talents reveal more of reality than what is perceived by a single individual, a dyad, or a triad. Shared perception generates higher levels of solutions to problems. Meanwhile, team spirit develops spontaneously parallel to authentic dialogue among team members. It is their courage to differ, their struggle to tackle differences and ultimately achieve consensus. The consensus which a group reaches after struggle enhances members' identification with the group and what it stands for. Even if the group fails to achieve consensus, a great deal of learning would have taken place. *Persisting to tackle challenges is far better than achieving consensus for the sake of maintaining equilibrium.* Equilibrium maintained by conformity pushes down intellectual functioning to its lowest level thus increasing the vulnerability of the social system in the face of future crises. A group exists to the extent that its members animate each other. Members must have the intention to enter into vital relationships with one another. They express themselves with the expectation to be criticized, corrected, or see their thoughts made use of and developed further by others.

What usually happens when the group fails?

First, *preaching more harmony and team spirit*. This reflects wishful thinking and would not be acceptable to intelligent and enterprising managers with long experience in business or government.

Second, the authoritarian solution: *authority takes over and imposes a solution as if the group has never existed*. This strategy is feasible if the group happened to belong to one organization. Often, the group may have been composed of members belonging to different organizations such as in negotiation teams representing. Furthermore, the long hours spent in authentic dialogue generates a great deal of invaluable insights which should not be wasted on account of one failure or a few failures. We should in the first place remember that the group is made up of individuals each of whom has unique life experiences and creative resources. The emergence of the group as a social entity does not lead to dilution of individual creativity. Meanwhile the group includes many possible dyads and triads that emerge in the course of the group's life. Even in a single meeting for few hours, we note that neither individuals nor simpler social structures (dyads and triads) vanish from existence. They are embedded there as possibilities that could be revived and used when the group fails. When a group fails, dissolution is not the only option. I propose using individuals or/and dyads, to have a shot at the dilemmas that the group failed to resolve.

Let me explain how I arrived at this proposal. What does an individual do, or should do, when faced with an insurmountable challenge? He or she reaches out for another individual to help. Now the problem is dealt with by a *dyad*. Similarly, when partners of a dyad fail to resolve intractable conflict, but would still hope to maintain the relationship, they call on a third party for help. Now the dyad has become a triad — a social setting which allows the activation of a role of mediation or arbitration. In both instances, what seemed unsolvable at one level could be solved through change to a higher level of social structure.

Let us now think along the same line in the case of a group facing a crisis that threatens discontinuation of the group. In the previous cases we moved from simple structures to more complex structures. In the case of the group, we move in the opposite direction, namely to single individuals or dyads. A useful technical term to label the change from a complex structure to a simpler structure is *devolution*. When a complex structure becomes unmanageable, it would be prudent to scale down to a simpler structure. Anyhow the individuals or dyads will be charged to do their homework away from the group, relying exclusively on their own resources. They would have fresh look on the issues which the group has failed to resolve. Naturally, the group would convene at a later date to receive the reports from the elected (or volunteered) individuals and dyads. In fact, all other members of the team would have thought through the same issues away from the group.

Changing the structure either from a simple structure to a more complex structure, or vice versa, is what actually happens in the case of large organizations. When faced with extinction or serious decline in competitive ability, corporations resort to *expansion* through mergers and acquisitions, or through divestiture, namely devolution, to smaller but more manageable structure. There are historical variations of the same phenomena at a national level. Bertrand Russell (1990)[32] provided convincing evidence of the validity of the theory I am proposing. He states:

> "The enlargement of the social unit must have been mainly the result of war. If two tribes had a war of extermination, the victorious tribe by the acquisition of new territory would be able to increase its numbers. *There would be an obvious advantage of an alliance of two or more tribes.* If the danger producing the alliance persisted, the alliance would, in time become an amalgamation. When a unit become too large for its members to know each other, there would come to be a need of some mechanism for arriving at collective decisions And this mechanism would inevitably develop by stages into something that a modern man would recognize as government." pp. 23–24

Russell refers to two conditions for survival of a large social system: one is enlargement of the social unit by the acquisition of new territory. The other is to develop by stages into a novel structure "that the modern man would recognize as government." Structural change, which we often hear about is neither *evolution* (expansion) nor *devolution* (scaling down). It

---

[32] Russell, Bertrand (1990). *Authority and the Individual.* London: Routledge (first published 1949).

usually consists of transforming a failing bureaucratic structure to a more complicated alternative. The rationale for the change is seldom spelled out clearly.

RUNNING MEETINGS

In the following space I will present a brief outline based on my experience; yet I am faced here with a major problem. That is that meetings vary significantly, each requiring different guidelines — for this reason, I am compelled to make my notes as generic as possible so that it would apply to different types of meetings. Consequently I will be brief, with hope that the practitioner would take this guideline as a generic model to be modified and elaborated to suit the nature of the groups he or she is in charge of.

1.   *Chairing a Meeting*

Communication with a group is dramatically different from talking to individuals. As the chairperson of a meeting, you must make conscious effort to shift your attention away from individuals and focus instead on the group as a collective entity. This of course requires prior knowledge of the basic parameters which define a group, and having an idea about the common phenomena to watch for, as the group process unfolds. In other words — you must position yourself, physically and mentally, in a way that enables you to see the group in its entirety. Your awareness of the group as your field of action will inevitably affect your conduct. For example, when you direct a question to a single individual, you will ascertain that all members have heard the question. On the other hand, if someone in the audience asks you question, you will make sure before replying that the question has been heard by all. You may for example, repeat the question. Better still, you may pose the question to the entire audience and request a reply before offering your own answer. Somehow, your recognition of the group as an entity will seep through the consciousness of the audience. The audience will spontaneously develop awareness that there is actually a group which transcends separate individuals. In the final analysis, the role of a chairperson is essentially to *steer the group process towards the attainment of a collective objective.* Your presence must always be felt by the group through your remarks, prodding, and timely intervention.

2.   *Commonality of the Objective*

Collective understanding of the objective is the chairperson's primary responsibility. The objective is an integrative force — but the objective may mean different things to different people. Therefore, as a chairperson, you should be alert to deviation from the target, implicit in interventions from the members of the group. It is then that your duty is to correct misinterpretation of the objective. Arguments and counter-arguments will show to what extent they are relevant to the group's mandate. The chairperson is the guardian of relevance. In fact, any member in the meeting should perform the same role; members have as much responsibility as the chairperson.

3.   *Composition*

The mandate of the group should determine the composition of the group. The composition varies with regard to diversity. There are objectives that call for a *highly specialized* group belonging to a certain discipline. Other tasks — such as strategic planning for the organization — require a *highly diversified* group, representing a wide range of specialties and skills. However, people belonging to the same discipline may have equal expertise, but certainly they have different views and different cognitive styles. Such differences are invaluable as far as the group performance is concerned. Equally important is whether members of the meeting belong to the same organization or to different organizations, such as in the case of negotiation. The dimension of homogeneity/diversity will determine the proper style for chairing the meeting.

4. *Formal Structure*

The following issues are to be considered:

a. Is there a need for assigned formal roles? Or let roles develop spontaneously as the meeting unfolds?

b. Should there be rules and procedures, such as voting on decisions or leave norms to develop spontaneously in the course of deliberation?

5. *Physical Environment*

Naturally the most important factor in the physical environment derives from our definition of a small group, namely the *interface* — the seating arrangement should:

a. Allow members to see and hear one another effortlessly;

b. To be seated comfortably next to each other; and

c. Be able to move around in their seats, or stand up when they feel like it.

Such details may sound trivial and need not be stressed. However, I cannot stress enough that sound thinking and emotional stability tend to be impeded by physical discomfort or space constraints.

6. *The Time Factor*

Participants need to know how much time they will spend in the meeting. However, there are contingencies that call for unexpected time extension or earlier adjournment. No meeting should interfere with other organizational or family commitments. Meanwhile, physical and mental tolerance must be monitored to decide on appropriate breaks. I need not point out the adverse effect of boredom and fatigue on problem-solving and decision-making, let alone how they lead to deterioration of human relations.

7. Emergence of Social Roles

As the meeting proceeds, you will note the emergence of roles that different members try to play. Roles can be identified in terms of relevance to the group agenda. We can briefly classify the roles into three categories:

a. Task related roles: serve the group objective and is consistent with the stated agenda.

b. Group maintenance roles: included in this category are behavior tendencies that serve the well-being of individuals — such as providing emotional support, encouragement, or alleviation of tension through humor or graceful gestures. Such roles may not be directly related to the group agenda, but they contribute to harmony and lift up group morale.

c. Self interest roles: or lobbying for special interest groups.

Spontaneous Structuring: as members watch each other, attractions and aversions will lead to development of dyads — both mutually supportive, and mutually competitive. Some dyads will crystallize and persist to the end. Others fade away while others evolve. Some dyadic structures will contribute to the mission of the group. Others will have the opposite effect; coalitions develop delaying consensus.

Conflict must be expected. Usually it starts as arguments and counter arguments over issues related to the meeting objectives. Every effort must be taken to keep it that way. Interventions must remain relevant to the mandate for which the meeting has been held.

8. Keep Track of Achievements

Consensus takes place gradually over separate issues. Every agreement should be recorded and reiterated. For this reason someone in the meeting should be assigned the role of summarizing what is going on in the meeting. Keeping track of the progress has a motivating influence on the group. Finally, the meeting should end abruptly — the chairperson or any other member, should report briefly on the issues considered by the group and conclude the report by clear statement of the outcome of the meeting: *what has been achieved, and what issues remain to be dealt with in future meetings.* Ideally, the verbal report at the end of the meeting should be followed by a more elaborate written report to be sent to the participants shortly after the meeting. The formalities I am suggesting here are intended to triumph over describing the tradition of meetings by such terms as *commititis.*

Indicators of success of a meeting:

1. More silence and more substance as the group develops
2. More readiness to agree than to object
3. More tendency to elaborate on contributions of other members

(For assessment of group performance, see Appendix: Group Analysis Form.)

CHAPTER SIX

WORK, PLAY AND LEISURE

SEMANTIC INTRODUCTION

The subject of *work, play and leisure* could not possibly be served properly as a brief portion of a book. It deserves an independent volume, if not an encyclopedia. However, for this book whose main concern is the *business of living*, I feel obligated to devote a space to it no matter how brief. I must at least clarify the role of this triad in the drama of human existence. In fact, *work, play and leisure* are implicit whenever we approach the subject of management. I cannot stress enough that management is essentially the business of taking charge of our life. The three components of this triad are equally necessary and important, as they sum up our existence in the world. Work may appear more important, but we will show later that the fate of work will depend on the worker's ability to shift attention to the other two. The central issue is the economy of energy, or balance in deployment of energy. So let us start by meanings of the words.

WORK VERSUS LABOR

As we embark on the subject of work in the life of humankind, we are confronted with a historical dilemma. That is the traditional differentiation between two notions, namely *work* and *labor*. We must get this semantic problem out of the way before we can freely tread this field. The differentiation came down from the ancient Greeks, who assigned labor to slaves and women in the household, whose concern has been the necessities of life, producing what is to be consumed almost immediately. In contrast, *free citizens* were assigned the task of governing. So the business of living was split into two major enterprises — labor for the disadvantaged, and politics for the elite who are fit to govern or lead. All the European words for 'labor', signify pain and effort: English *labor*, the Greek *panos*, the French *travail*, the German *arbeit*. Labor is also used for the pangs of birth. The function of labor is subsisting, doing what the human body needs in order to respond to the necessities of life. Thus, labor has traditionally been considered the lowest level of man's activity. But exceptions did happen. Hanna Arendt (1958)[33] traced the rise of the concept of labor from "the lowest, most despised position to the highest rank, as the most esteemed of human activities." She notes that three philosophers were responsible for this rise. First, John Locke when he saw that labor is the source of all property. The second is Adam Smith who identified labor as the source of all wealth. The third is Karl Marx. Marx considered labor the source of all productivity and the expression of the very humanity of man. Marx considered labor to be "the supreme world-building capacity of man," to use Arendt's expression.

Two notions stand out in how Marx viewed labor:

---

[33] Arendt, H. (1958). *The human condition.* Chicago: The University of Chicago Press.

a. Labor is nature's expression of the human person at the most
    primitive level. And being primitive does not necessarily mean
    inferior.

b. Labor enables the human person to participate in creating the world
    and continuing the process of life. Marx expressed this point very
    succinctly by calling labor "man's metabolism with nature."

Now that we have removed this semantic obstacle, we are confronted with
another one, also semantic in nature. That is the differentiation between
work as *activity*, and work as *product of activity*. For instance, when we
talk about works of a writer or an artist, we are really referring to his or
her products of *working*. The nouns *work* (English), *oeuvre* (French), and
werk (German) are generally used for works of art in all three languages
and may be in many other languages as well. My concern in this section of
the book is work as *human activity*. Meanwhile, I consider the dichotomy
work of the body versus work of the mind a historical remnant that modern
technological and scientific developments render obsolete. In fact,
whatever we do with our body involves mental processes of sensation,
space and time perception, memory, and other cognitive processes.
Mental and bodily processes *interpenetrate*, as it were. Even the simplest
function, like seeing, is impossible without movement of the eye ball and
the head. Furthermore, the whole body changes its position in the
person's deliberate effort to apprehend the optical field. Then, there is
looking, a voluntary act driven by the need to know clearly. Evolution of
technology over the years gave rise to ever increasing professions or
specialized occupations. Furthermore, the dichotomy *body-work* versus
mind-work, is imbued with ideological value judgment which runs counter
to scientific thinking.[34] I therefore choose not to separate work as activity,
from work as product of activity. They could be separated conceptually,
but not in reality.

---

[34] Manual work implies, and serves cognition. Recent studies of cognitive processes underlying
motor behavior.

FUNCTION OF WORK

The first question that comes to mind is: *what is the function of work in the life of humans?* My spontaneous response is that work is the natural affirmation of man's existence in the world. Indeed, humans like animals, have nowhere to survive except in the environment. They are biologically destined to live in relation to the world. But the world is not in a state of chaos, it consists of dynamic ecological systems. It follows that an ecological perspective is not only helpful in understanding work, but is also necessary. Man's existence in the world is a question of reciprocal interaction between human's bio-psycho-social systems and the ecological systems of the environment. Gibson's[35] concept of *affordance* establishes the connection. The environment *affords* animals such necessities for existence as terrain, shelters, tools, and other animals. Animals are biologically equipped with the ability to seek what the environment has to afford. J.J. Gibson (1979/1986) invented the noun *affordance* because it stresses the mutuality of animal and environment which no other noun can. An *affordance* relates attributes of something in the environment to an agent who has some ability to perceive what the environment has to offer. Affordances (in the environment) and abilities or aptitudes (of the living species) explain the inevitable interaction between the living agent and the environment.

The ecological approach applies equally to animals and humans. However, humans' potentialities to perceive (and exploit) affordances far exceed the adaptive potential (mostly instinctive) of any animal species. Man does not simply insert himself into the environment and becomes part of it. Rather, man enters into relations with the environment which includes nature and other animal species. The interface with the ecological systems is inevitable. Humans have the impulse or the urge to explore the existing affordances, adapt to them, and exploit them. As the ecologist would say, an organism needs to "see clearly, to hear distinctly" so as to

---

[35] Gibson, J. J. (1979). *The Ecological Approach to Visual Perception.* Boston: Houghton Mifflin. Reprinted 1986, Erlbaum.

cope adequately with environmental events. Moreover, humans soon realize that nature does not account for every contingency. Curiosity about environmental opportunities, forces, and dangers is intrinsic motivation in humans. Motivation is much broader than the concept of *work motivation* we psychologists spend so much time and effort theorizing and experimenting about. Exploratory behavior has been detected in human subjects as early as infancy. That is how humans, whether as individuals or structured in groups, use ingenuity and imagination to devise artificial means to satisfy their needs. So while they capitalize upon available resources (affordances), they explore possibilities. Furthermore, they differ from animals by virtue of historicity. They are *time-bound*, to use Korzybski's expression. They have a past to build on and a future to realize. They pass over their accomplishments to future generations. That is how human cultures develop as a historical process of accumulation.

One point is worth stressing here, namely, that man changes the environment by acting upon it through work. By changing the environment, man changes himself. In short, man complements nature. As we indicated in a previous chapter, man is a social force in the environment. It is within this framework that I place "work, play, and leisure." Existing in the world is more than securing a place in it such as the case with animals. Meanwhile, we must bear in mind that the environment is neither static nor inert. Suffice it to think of rain, thunder, earthquakes, tsunamis, suffocating heat or freezing cold, wind or storms, fertility or aridity of soil, and so on and so forth. So much for the human agent constitute affordances to exploit, to benefit from, or avoid. While there are ferocious beasts to avoid or hunt, there are animals to domesticate and benefit from in terms of food, as vehicles of transportation, or as domestic companions.

The need to know the world is primary or intrinsic motive. A corollary of this motive is another equally intrinsic need, namely, competence. Competence is sought through learning. We are naturally endowed with memory which enables us to build on past experience, to improve our skills. Thus, our skills evolve from primitive means of survival to highly sophisticated technical means. Competence is reached through designing ever evolving technology to maximize the utilization of our energies and using our energies in exploring hidden energies in the natural world. Skill is a construct, a system of integrated components — perceptual, physical, intellectual and moral. Naturally, those components coalesce though with different degrees of participation in the whole depending on the ultimate objective of the work. None of these components is absent in any skill whether we call it *intellectual, physical* or *social*. We can apply any of these adjectives preceded by the adverb, "predominantly." For example, smooth swimming could be called *predominantly* physical, but not entirely so.

MORALITY AND PROFESSIONAL MASTERY

Any skill is regulated by emotive restraint, perseverance and self control. There is also the feature of harmony, sense of responsibility, discipline, and good taste. This applies equally to intellectual, as well as to what might be considered essentially physical skill. For instance, scientific research demands absolute sincerity and moral constraint. A true scientist does not set out to prove a hypothesis. A scientist has first to examine the opposite hypothesis, the *null hypothesis*. In other words, the starting point in scientific enquiry is self criticism, considering the plausibility of the opposite opinion. This is essentially a moral position. John Stuart Mill (2007)[36] is very clear about the moral stance that regulates scientific enquiry. He tells us:

> "He who knows only his own side of the case knows little of that. His reasons may be good, and no one may have been able to refute them. But if he is equally unable to refute the reasons on the opposite side, if he does not so much as know what they are, he has no ground for preferring either opinion.

[36] Mill, John Stuart. (2007). *On Liberty*. USA: Pearson Education (first published 1806).

The rational position for him would be suspension of judgment, and unless he contents himself with that, he is either led by authority or adopts, like the generality of the world, the side to which he feels most inclination. Nor is it enough that he should hear the arguments of adversaries from his own teachers, presented as they state them, and accompanied by what they offer as refutations. This is not the way to do justice to the arguments or bring them into real contact with his own mind. He must be able to hear them from persons who actually believe them, who defend them in earnest and do their very utmost for them. He must know them in their most plausible and persuasive form; he must feel the whole force of the difficulty which the true view of the subject has to encounter and dispose of, [or] else he will never really possess himself of the portion of truth which meets and removes that difficulty." p. 95 [my emphasis]

Mill lays down the moral principles for scientific enquiry: *courage to assume refutability of one's opinion no matter how strong the reasons, diligence to explore the validity of the opposite opinion.* In the examination of the opposite opinion, Mill demands that we consider the most powerful arguments in favor of the opposite opinion. It is no accident that sciences are called disciplines. That is in the intellectual sphere, but morality is also involved in what we might consider manual labor. I cite the example of carpentry from my experience as adolescent. There was a carpenter in my neighborhood in Alexandria, Egypt. He became a close friend despite our difference of age. He was a grown adult. The only thing we had in common was that he had received elementary education from the same school I had recently graduated from. I looked up to him as a mentor. Nevertheless, he treated me as he would treat a person of his age. His workshop consisted of one room which opened directly to the street. He placed two chairs on the side-walk for potential visitors or clients. I would spend hours seated while he is toiling with remarkable perseverance and dedication.

What impressed me most, besides his dedication and perseverance was his tendency to pause to tell a story, or comment on the events of war that was raging at the time (WWII). Work was sustained thanks to his leisurely style. I very much enjoyed witnessing the emergence of a piece of furniture from the beginning to the end. I knew then that working is synonymous with creating. How can I describe my reaction watching a master at work? My reaction could not be described by a single word. It is just too complex, as complex as the human craft we call carpentry. Instead, a concatenation of adjectives spring up in my mind — discipline, precision, good taste, perseverance, and joy of creation. Such conglomerate of noble qualities may explain the air of dignity bestowed upon a craftsman or master of any trade at work. It is not surprising that Christ spent several years doing carpentry which he learnt from St. Joseph.

It is clear from the above that through work, man is driven by a natural need to be an active agent in the world. The carpenter takes tools and materials from the physical environment, knowledge and training from masters who are also among the *affordances* in the environment. The carpenter uses body and mind in transforming wood, formerly a living tree, to a product which will be used by human clients in the same social environment. A complex pattern of relationships is evident.

But let us get away from personal reminiscences and sentimental indulgence and revert to technology at a more general level. I must first remind the reader that I view the development of technology as a function of historical interaction between man's bio-psycho-social systems and the ecological systems of the environment. A. Rapoport (1983)[37] distinguishes four technological systems or "phyla" as Rapoport calls them. Rapoport borrowed the term *phylum* from the field of biology where a phylum is a primary subdivision of a category grouping together all classes of organisms that have the same body plan. The four phyla (or systems) of technology which Rapoport has identified are briefly defined below:

[37] Rapoport, A. Technological models of the nervous system. *ETC: A Review of General Semantics*, Vol. 40, No. 3, 1983, pp. 312–324.

1. *Tools*

    Tools appear functionally as extensions of our limbs and they serve primarily for transmitting forces which originate in our own muscles.

2. *Clockworks*

    A clockwork is wound up, that is, potential mechanical energy is stored in it, which may be released at an arbitrary later time and/or over a prolonged period of time.

3. *Heat Engines*

    As with tools and clockworks, the output of the heat engine is an output of energy which had been put into it. But whereas the energy put into the earlier classes of machines was in the form of mechanical stress, which is obviously associated with our own muscular effort, the energy put into a heat engine is contained in a fuel. No muscular effort is apparent. Fuel is simply 'fed' to the heat engine.

4. *Information*

    The machines of the fourth phylum are primarily concerned with systematizing operations in which utilization of energy is involved. The "power" of these machines is not "muscular" power but "mental." The giants among them are capable of receiving, transmitting, and storing complex sets of directions, i.e., large amounts of "information." These machines simulate not muscular effort but human intelligence.

Let us ponder the implications of technological evolution as presented by Rapoport. We may arrive at a number of conclusions:

First, *progress of technology is presented as successive modes of utilization of human energy.* The first attempt of man to survive was reliance on sheer physical energy regulated of course by mental abilities. Very early, man discovered that his force can be augmented by the use of tools. The discovery of tools increased man's competence, or if you prefer, effectiveness. But, as Rapoport has indicated, every successive phase in technological progress implies less exertion of physical force until we end with total reliance on intellectual capabilities. The material used in the last phase, or phylum, to be loyal to Rapoport's vocabulary, is the stage of information. The skill at this stage is the mental effort of organizing information — fast access to information, organizing and effective exchange of information.

Second, *technology does not exist in isolation.* It exists in social and cultural environment. Technology was destined to become a force that alters the environment. It is true that a new product may be invented by individuals, but is soon diffused and used by social structures such as corporations, governments and various other societal institutions. The final outcome of technology development depends to a great extent on how we manage technology and the structures of institutions built around it. We soon realize that organizational effectiveness fails to match technological levels of creativity. At this point we are confronted with the bitter fact that organizational ability lags behind scientific innovation and the resulting technological advance.

Third, *information technologies alter power relations.* The new technologies change the way the information flows through a company and some executives interpret these changes as a challenge to their authority in the corporate hierarchy. I might add that technology altered power relations in the political arena as well, and in favor of the younger generations. The young generations surpassed their parents (and seniors in general) in catching up with information technology.

Fourth, not unlike medicine, *technological feats have its negative side effects.* They boost man's confidence which may at one point foster the illusion of omnipotence. Excessive need for control may blind human individuals and groups as to the destructive effect of some technologies on the health of the environment, another manifestation of the fact that organization management may lag behind technological progress.

Fifth, *specialization led to proliferation of professions or occupations.* We do not talk about jobs any more, but about careers. The notion of career brings the factor of long term to the life of workers. Instead of choosing a job, trained individuals seek a career that structures their entire working life. The value of specialization is short-lived due to shortened longevity of technology. This in turn presents organizations and individual professionals with the problem of obsolescence. In other words, past experience, acquired knowledge, and skills becoming irrelevant. That leads to further need for perpetual education.

I would like to stress at this point the fact that scientific and technological progress is far ahead of our ability to organize and make the most out of this progress. Failure in organization is evident in deterioration of working conditions, which may abort the potential advantages gained from technological progress.

It may be appropriate at this point to cite some manifestations of the serious consequences of organizational context of work.

According to a report by the World Labor Organization, 270 million employees are victims of work accidents and 160 million contract professional diseases. The study also shows that the number of people who die during the exercise of their jobs exceeds 20 million every year. This means that work kills 5000 personnel per day.[38] Writes Ignacio Ramonet in *Le Monde Diplomatique*, June 2003, "according to the National Chamber of Medical Assurance, 780 employees are killed by work (2 per day), not to mention that this figure is an underestimate." He adds, "1,350,000 work accidents. This means there are 3,700 victims every single day. In other words, 8 employees are involved in accidents for every working day of 8 hours." This is the *blood price* paid for the sake of growth and competition.

We talk about management styles, job satisfaction, work motivation, leadership effectiveness. None of these studies take into consideration the effect of all these conditions on the mental health of the workers and customers, let alone societies in which the organizations perform. We seem to conceal the issue of sanity as a taboo. We talk about counseling rather than mental health of the executive and the relevance of organizational polices and management style of bosses to mental health of the constituency and the communities at large. When we attribute

---

[38] Quoted by *Le Monde Diplomatique*, Internet version of June 2003.

ineffectiveness to a style of management, we rarely see it as a function of failure in the emotional stability of the manager. We consider the self defeating quality as lack of skill or lack of awareness. Often the style reflects emotional instability or failure in social adjustment. Occasionally it is a function of outright mental illness, neurosis or even worse. Furthermore a style has an effect on subordinates' sense of well being. The same applies to the emotional stability of a group of workers. Morale of the group can affect the emotional stability of the manager, particularly if the manager were naturally vulnerable. Influence flows in both directions.

The many problems occurring at work may explain (but does not necessarily justify) anti-work movement around the world. I site two examples of champions against work. I came across two bestsellers that reflect this tune-out culture: Corinne Maier's *Bonjour Paresse* (*Good Morning Laziness* in France) and Tom Hodgkinson's *How to Be Idle* in Britain. Both authors advise that the route to sanity is to do as little as possible in your job while saving yourself for your *real life* outside the work-place. Anti-work slogans abound. One slogan sticks in my mind, "work less to produce more."

But the anti-work movement is understandable reaction to organizational failures, however, it could not obliterate the inherent value of work, nor does it deny the reality of work as an essential mode of existence. Work structures the life of the worker and brings order to his or her daily life. In the process, the worker develops and experiences the privilege of being useful to the family and society at large. That is crucial for instilling self-esteem. We would be impressed by the psychological value of work if we ponder the destructive effect of unemployment on the integrity of the human person. Daily contacts provide invaluable experiences to each individual who engages genuinely in group life. In short, work itself facilitates the experience of becoming. The French proverb, "l'oisiveté est la mère de tous les vices" states it well, in other words, *l'oisiveté — the condition of having no work — is the mother (cause) of all vices*. Unemployment is a source of poverty, but also a sense of *uselessness to the world* causing great social suffering. Work still largely determines the standard of living through the income it provides and is the basis of personal identity and social status. Inevitably work is also the source of social divisions between leaders and performers, skilled and unskilled, rich and poor.

PLAY

We cannot possibly solve the problems pertaining to work without bringing in the subject of play and leisure. As we intimated earlier *work, play and leisure* are dynamically inter-related. But let us first see what play means. The question we pose as a start is: *what distinguishes work from play?* Peter Loizos (1980)[39] discussed the play phenomenon from the standpoint of images of man. He dealt with the contrast between work and play as reflection of misunderstanding. The perceived contrast between work and play is summarized in the table below.

TABLE: 4

Perceptions of Work and Play

WORK	PLAY
obligatory	voluntary
tiring	refreshing
disciplined	spontaneous
hierarchical	egalitarian
serious	not serious
formal	informal
done for others	done for oneself

The list of characteristics often ascribed to work implies that work is unpleasant and coercive activity. The words describing play in the right column have a positive ring. Loizos argues that the contrast is highly

[39] Loizos, P. (1980). Images of man. In J. Cherfas, and R. Lewin, (Eds.) *Not Work Alone: A Cross-cultural View of Activities Superfluous to Survival.* Beverly Hills, California: Sage Publications. pp. 231–247.

misleading. He notes that people with a high degree of work satisfaction tend to emphasize the voluntary, refreshing, and self-directed nature of what they do. They report moments of spontaneity. Someone plagued with a boring, repetitive job would probably agree to all the qualities listed in the left hand column; yet for others work is unreal and play is real, work the non-serious way of filling up time between serious bouts of play. We see the basic terms very much through our own experiences, and the peculiarities of advanced industrial societies, in which so many tasks lack any intrinsic reward, and do not seem directly and immediately related to meeting one's immediate needs.

As Loizos has indicated, a great deal of what goes on at work is not work. There is joking, horse-play, courtship, making friends, and all sorts of devices to relieve boredom. Work has been differentiated from play by the fact that the former tends to be hierarchical, whereas the social structure in play tends to be egalitarian. In fact, games are often hierarchical in their internal organization, with captains, and expert specialists for particular tasks, which make them like *work-teams*. Loizos refers to William Whyte's study of *Street Corner Society*, a study of young men who stood about on a street corner in downtown Boston:

> "Whyte observed that Doc, the informal but undisputed leader of the gang, used to win remarkably often when the group went to the bowling alley; while this was partly a matter of personal skill, it was also influenced by the way his lieutenants and he himself behaved when junior members of the group were taking their turns. A good deal of caustic mockery was directed at the subordinates, which made it psychologically harder for them to bowl well, whereas when Doc bowled, the group not only expected him to do well, and refrained from catcalling, but actually cheered him on." pp. 237–238

I must add an important observation to the critique put forward by Loizos. Any job is a complex entity that consists of several component tasks which differ with regard to several dimensions: difficulty, degree of reliance on mechanical repetitiveness, versus reliance on judgment. They also differ with regard to the degree of satisfaction or stress they provide. Meanwhile workers vary with regard to tolerance of boredom. Workers also differ with regard to work habits. We cannot talk about work in the abstract, but about work as activities by individuals and groups. So the quality of seriousness as a property of work depends on the characteristics of those who do the work.

Sometimes play is regarded as a very serious affair. For instance, children are dead serious about what we consider frivolous play. Sports are considered as play, but once adults engage in a game, it becomes a serious affair and winning or losing makes a difference. Furthermore, no matter how dedicated a person is, total immersion in a task for a prolonged time cuts the person off from surroundings and gets him/her servile to what he or she is doing. Boredom and sometimes sense of helplessness ensues. In judging the difference between work and play, we must realize that each constitutes a complex process which could not be judged globally. Take for example, learning to play a sport such as tennis or golf. The early stage has the quality of hard work with intermittent feelings of discouragement and thoughts of quitting. But once competence in playing has been reached, pleasure of playing compensates for past experiences of struggle.

Availability for opportunity to play during the working day is much more effective than waiting to play in the weekend. It would even be more effective if opportunities for play present themselves as soon as fatigue is reached, or as soon as boredom sets in. Many organizations have been sensitive to this factor and included in the design of work place areas where employees can practice sports or workout, shower and return to work refreshed and motivated. The refreshing effect of play when needed is indeed remarkable. This does not of course deny the value of more elaborate engagement in sports during the weekends or vacations.

LEISURE

What then is leisure? We can learn about leisure from individuals who are deprived of it. They get immersed at work and cannot liberate themselves from its tyranny. I counseled few doctorate students who experienced crises of mental blocking as they struggle with the last stages of dissertation writing. They do not dare to quit and seem to engage in a battle with their own minds. These crises of mental blocking are quite frequent in the lives of writers and artists. My advise to these intellectuals is usually to stop the struggle, get away from stubborn fighting and do something else. I remember listening to Nehru, the Indian leader in London when I was a graduate student. He was addressing Indian students. He told the students that one cannot think properly unless he gains the experience of doing manual work. Somehow, he thought, changing the nature of activity provides relief and clarity to the stressed intellectual worker. Nehru did not mention the word leisure, but that is how I interpret the function of shifting from intellectual to manual activity. The mind does not stop functioning, but gets the rest it needs. Meanwhile, the energy flows into other regions of the mind. Intellectual blockage or inhibition crisis is a very frustrating condition. The intellectual is in effect incarcerated in one compartment of the self. He cannot afford quitting the ongoing activity, but at the same time is unable to make any progress. He or she is locked up in conflict with his own mind. He turns around in circles. The more he thinks the more mired he gets. My ready advice to doctorate candidates was simple: "Let go, stop fighting, your brain will not yield. You are cut off from your surroundings. You need fresh air and return home, to your entire self." I add, "This is not yielding or giving up. It is a break to replenish your energy which has been sapped by circular thinking. Let the energy flow into other avenues until the whole system is restored." Some counselees returned to work with vigor to accomplish what they had set out to achieve. Others discovered to their surprise and delight that they did not in the first place like what they were doing and changed the course adopting another topic of studies or pursued a totally different course. It seems that under certain circumstance, doing nothing as an act of will can be liberating.

We can appreciate the wisdom of leisure by watching animal species *doing nothing* after periods of intense activity. Some scientists strenuously object to the use of the term laziness to describe any animal behavior, which they say implies some willful shirking of a task. They found out that animals are inactive when they have to be. It's not as though they are choosing to be at rest. In a fascinating article by Angier (1991)[40], he tells us that some biologists are beginning to shift the focus of their research. Rather than observing the behavior of animals in action, as field researchers historically have, they are attempting to find out the many factors that lie behind animal inertia. (pp. C1, C10)

Some concrete examples selected from Angier's account would clarify the value of leisure as a survival strategy:

1. A lion can lie in the same spot without budging, for 12 hours at a stretch... [lions] are active on their feet maybe two or three hours. In that brief spate of effort, they are likely to be either hunting or devouring the booty of that hunt, which is one reason they need so much down time... Their bellies get extremely fat, and they look incredibly uncomfortable and incredibly immobile, lying on their backs and panting in the heat.

2. Many species of monkeys sit around as much as three-quarters of the day, not to mention the 12 hours of the night they usually spend sleeping.

3. Moose are ruminants, like cattle, and must stay fairly still while digesting food. For every hour of grazing on vegetation, the moose needs four hours to metabolize its food. It has to rest.

4. Several hundred species of mammals go into hibernation each winter cutting down on energy expenditure, lowering their metabolic rates.

---

[40]Angier, N. (July 30, 1991). As busy as a bee. *The New York Times*.

We also learn that underlying the inactivity of some animal species is social arrangement to preserve the overall energy of the species. For example, some animals appear to be sleeping, but they are just maintaining quiet vigilance. Such a need for vigilance may help explain why bees and ants spend so much time resting. Honey bees have a soldier caste; members do little or nothing around the hive, but they are the first to act should the hive be disturbed. "They are like a standing army — they are hanging around the colony, not doing anything in particular, but they can be immediately mobilized." Other bees and ants may be saving their energy for a big job, like discovery of an abundant new source of food, which requires overtime effort to harvest it, or the intermittent splitting of the one hive into two, which suddenly leaves fewer workers to do the same tasks. A colony has a labor force bigger than it really needs to get through those critical episodes. Says Angier:

> "Studies show that social insects cannot afford to waste their energy on non-critical activities. It turns out ants and bees are born with a set amount of energy to devote to their colony, which for reasons that remain mysterious seems to have less to do with the amount of food they eat than with an inborn genetic program. They have a fixed amount of energy in them, which they can use up quickly or slowly. The harder they work, the quicker they die."

It is remarkable how a species is predisposed to consider not only the limits of individual energy, but the fate of energy of the total community. I believe that this could, and should be done, by humans as well. But we need to invent it, because instinct in human species does not provide a ready solution to this problem. In fact, the example below shows that there is so much that we can do. This is a daring decision taken by the governor of Utah that has been lauded by the all employees of the state. Johann Hari reported the story in *The Independent*, London (2010):[41]

---

[41] "We don't need this culture of overwork." *The Independent*, London. January 9, 2010.

"It all began two years ago, when the state [Utah] was facing a budget crisis. One night, the new Republican Governor Jon Huntsman was staring at the red ink and rough sums when he had an idea. Keeping the state's buildings lit and heated and manned cost a fortune. Could it be cut without cutting the service given to the public? Then it hit him. What if, instead of working 9 to 5, Monday to Friday, the state's employees only came in four days a week, but now from 8 to 6? The state would be getting the same forty hours a week from its staff — but the costs of maintaining their offices would plummet. The employees would get a three-day weekend, and cut a whole day's worth of tiring, polluting commuting out of their week. He took the step of requiring it by law for 80 per cent of the state's employees. (Obviously, some places, like the emergency services or prisons, had to be exempted.) At first, there was cautious support among the workforce but as the experiment has rolled on, it has gathered remarkable acclaim. Today, two years on, 82 per cent of employees applaud the new hours, and hardly anyone wants to go back. Professor Lori Wadsworth carried out a detailed study of workers' responses, and she says: *"People love it."*

It seems that an order that has been in place for years tends to be taken by people who surrendered to it as a natural order if not a fate. It is easier to perpetuate a habit or custom than face the uncertainty of a new order no matter how liberating it may turn out to be. It takes a champion who dares to challenge the common wisdom. Naturally, in the case above, the champion happened to be the Governor himself backed by his legal authority. He was also lucky that the decision was welcome by the constituency for the very simple reason it increased the time available for leisure, without reducing the time for work.

ARISTOTLE'S VIEW

I think we must be clear by now that self management demands that *work, play, and leisure* should be dealt with as a *system*. We get more clarity about this issue from a quote I came across in the Aristotle classic, 'Politics'. In this quote Aristotle contrasted the three notions of work, play, and leisure to each other. He also demonstrated how the three sets of activities complement each other. Rather than impose my analysis of Aristotle's view, I produce the quote dealing with the three notions below. Let me first preface that Aristotle defined the three notions within his overall philosophy of education. The chief aim of education according to him is "to enable the citizen to employ his intellectual and artistic faculties to the full, to live a life of *virtue* and of *leisure.*" Let us first present the quote in its entirety:

> "If we need both work and leisure, but the latter is preferable to the former and is its end, we must ask ourselves what are the proper activities of leisure. Obviously not play; for that would inevitably be to make play our end in life, which is impossible. Play has its uses, but they belong rather to the sphere of work; for he who toils needs rest, and play is a way of resting, while work is inseparable from toil and strain. We must therefore admit play, but keeping it to its proper uses and occasions, and prescribing it as a cure; such movement of the soul is a relaxation, and because we enjoy it, rest."

Aristotle then goes on to spell out the unique function of leisure contrasting it with work. He brings in the factor of pleasure and happiness:

> "But leisure seems in itself to contain pleasure, happiness and the blessed life. This is a state attained not by those at work but by those at leisure, because he that is working is working for some hitherto unattained end and happiness is an end... Admittedly, men do not agree as to what that pleasure is; each

man decides for himself following his own disposition, the best
man choosing the best kind of enjoyment from the finest
sources. Thus it becomes clear that, in order to spend leisure in
civilized pursuits, we do require a certain amount of learning
and education, and that these branches of education and these
subjects studied must have their own intrinsic purpose, as
distinct from those necessary occupational subjects which are
studied for reasons beyond themselves."

Aristotle brings in the subject of necessity, usefulness or utility of
different types of human pursuits. Again, he ends by showing how
pursuits in leisure should be different.

"Hence, in the past, men laid down music as part of education,
not as being necessary, for it is not in that category, nor yet as
being useful in the way that a knowledge of reading and
writing is useful for business or household administration,
for study, and for many of the activities of a citizen, nor as a
knowledge of drawing seems useful for the better judging of
the products of a skilled worker, nor again as gymnastic is
useful for health and vigor — neither of which do we see
gained as a result of music. There remains one purpose — for
civilized pursuits during leisure; and that is clearly the reason
why they do introduce it, for they give it a place in what they
regard as the civilized pursuits of free men.

It is also clear that there are some useful things, too, in
which the young must be educated, not only because they are
useful (for example they must learn reading and writing), but
also because they are often the means to learning yet further
subjects. Similarly they must learn drawing, not for the sake
of avoiding mistakes in private purchases, and so that they
may not be taken in when buying and selling utensils, but
rather because it teaches one to be observant of physical
beauty. But to be constantly asking 'What is the use of it?' is

unbecoming to those of broad vision and unworthy of free men." pp. 455–457

WHAT DO WE LEARN FROM ARISTOTLE?

First, *work consists of activities which are inherently painful* — "inseparable from toil and strain." But since work is necessary, Aristotle introduces play as rest or cure. He characterizes play as enjoyable "movement of the soul." He establishes the psychological balance through the alternation of work and play.

Second, *Aristotle acknowledges man's need for pleasure which could be attained by leisure.* He identifies the pleasure attained by leisure as "civilized pursuits" which must be "culturally elevated." He considers leisure inherently different from both work in two respects: first, it does not seek an end beyond itself; second, it is subject to free choice. Says Aristotle, "each man decides for himself, following his own disposition — the best man choosing the best kind of enjoyment from the finest sources."

Aristotle treats *work, play and leisure* as distinct, and yet complementary activities. This projects a humanistic model of the human person whose existence in the world should be characterized by balance and harmony. It is a shame that a genius such as Aristotle failed to counter a culture that did not extend the model to slaves and women who should toil in the household while free men govern as citizens.

WHAT CAN WE ADD TO ARISTOTLE?

Aristotle defined leisure as activities which are inherently different from either work or play. However, I submit that leisure could also be a property of any activity. For instance, a worker enjoys the pleasure of work progressing smoothly, without being harassed by time or constant worry about the outcome in terms of specific return. Such blissful experience is possible only if the worker happened to be his own master, and free to pace himself or herself.

We should not however, lose sight of the fact that there are many people who welcome imposed structure of work, provided the roles are clearly defined, and the rules are consistent, fair and functional. Well-organized activities provide predictability, clarity and sense of order. Workers are grateful when they receive guidance and are enabled to experience progression towards well-conceived objectives. In this light we can understand the fear workers experience as retirement approaches. Free time then looms as a threatening void.

During a visit to a bank in Alexandria, Egypt, officials in one department told me that it is a common custom that pensioners pay frequent visits to their former colleagues during working hours. They often drop by to sip coffee and chat with their former colleagues. While the former workers enjoy the visits out of nostalgia to *the good old times* of working, their hosts do not really appreciate the interruption, but conceal their feelings out of courtesy and respect for custom. It may very well be that those unwelcome visitors have realized the blessings of work life though in retrospect. Could it be that the pull of a working environment has become a form of leisure or rest which alleviates the stress of the dreary existence of retirement?

One of the drawbacks of retirement is that it marks a shift from structured work activities with high degree of predictability to an unstructured life. Typically, the retiree must engage in disparate activities that tend to be menial by comparison to skilled activities at work. That is of course, in case the retired person does not secure a second career. The retiree lacks the umbrella of an institution or office where he or she assumes a distinct role (or roles) in effecting long-term projects. It is not only working which the retiree misses. Rather it is the living in an orderly and vibrant environment.

I might add that retirement alters the dynamics of the family. Both the retired person and the family must adapt to novel circumstances that are not always welcome. A high-level executive told me that upon retirement his wife told him "From now on, I will have to deal with double husband and half salary." The wife was of course joking. Nevertheless, the joke has a ring of truth, and the truth is that retirement seems to be a dramatic change not only for the retired person, but also for his or her family. Of course there are other families who wait for retirement with well designed plans to enjoy the leisure of retirement years.

Let us go back to work under normal circumstances and see what individuals can do to reduce work stress. Naturally, we cannot adequately cover the problem of work stress in the remainder of this chapter. Suffice it to mention a few highlights.

ENERGY MANAGEMENT

We learn from Aristotle as well as from studies of animal species, that *work, play, and leisure* are related modes of energy deployment. The worker is well advised to remember that the primary property of energy is the tendency to flow in any direction. You cannot suppress energy, but you can channel it in the pursuit of one or the other goal.

Energy could be deployed in the following ways:

- in a mental operation,
- in a sensory manual task,
- in emotional expression,
- or in all of these reactions combined.

Energy could be either *kinetic*, when it is in the process of being discharged in movement, whether mental or physical. Or it could be *potential*, when stored for future use.

Competent workers learn that vitality over the long term is not indicated by how much energy is expended at a given moment in time, but *how much energy is kept in store*. Perseverance depends on having high energy level, but it also depends on economic utilization of energy and availability of energy to maintain continuity of effort. The differentiation seems obvious but some workers may lack, or ignore this knowledge.

A young manager once told me: "if by the end of a working day I do not feel exhausted, I know that I did not do a good job." This manager was a rising star in his organization. He was probably seduced by achievement and aspires to achieve more. We may guess that his supervisors welcome his *dynamism*. But how long can he sustain this level of exertion day in and day out? In fact, he may manifest the same level of *dynamism* in working-out in the gym during the weekend, which means that the same compulsion of hard work extends to sports. Playing in this case would cease to be *play* since it acquires the harshness of *work*. The situation is worsened by the fact that leisure had no place in this man's life.

Management of energy entails deliberate effort to monitor how we expend our energy in a given task. While accomplishing a task, the worker should be sensitive to incoming messages from different parts of his or her body as well as from the mind. Effectiveness of energy management is indicated by the worker's early anticipation of exhaustion. The manager then would spontaneously slow down before reaching the point of being totally exhausted. There is also a social factor a worker must be aware of, namely that one's energy impacts the people with whom the worker interacts in any cooperative or competitive enterprise. Often enthusiasm beyond a certain level of intensity, exhilarating as it is to the worker, may have a draining effect on co-workers.

JOB SATISFACTION AND JOB STRUCTURE

There has been much talk about job satisfaction, a quality of global experience of the totality of a job. This is of course welcome, but it ignores the fact that a job is not a dense undifferentiated entity. Any job is a dynamic process that consists of different tasks involving different mental and physical functions, ranging from the most primitive to the most sophisticated. Furthermore, a job is a historical process of successive phases culminating in a desired output. The output could be a product, or an act that will impact the world in one way or another. Meanwhile performing a job may require exchange between different co-workers. This adds the burden of interpersonal communication, resolving contradictions, and building up consensus. Meanwhile, successive phases of a job do not necessarily proceed in a linear fashion. More often than not, the need may arise for reversal of decisions or taking a step backwards to change direction and opt for different paths towards the desired end or newly conceived ends. Different components and phases of a job vary with regard to difficulty, or with regard to the degree of satisfaction it provides the working person.

Hence, in the importance of understanding job structure: the worker must be able to analyze his or her job into its constituent components and phases with the view of finding out:

a. how these components relate to each other;

b. the demands each component makes on different personality resources;

c. your attitude towards each whether positive or negative;

d. the challenge each represents to you.

Some components of the job may be boring because they demand mechanical attention to details. Others are challenging and boosting of morale. The mood changes as a worker proceeds from a phase of the job to the next. In conclusion, we cannot expect all aspects or all phases of a job to be uniformly exciting. But what is important is the worker's appreciation of the value of the job and its meaningfulness relative to his or her life project. It follows that tolerance of boredom and respect of menial tasks as necessary ingredients of the job are prerequisites for overall work satisfaction.

Going back to energy management, the question arises, *what if the worker for some reason does not have sufficient energy?* In case of reduced energy or frequent fatigue, one can still accomplish work, though in small installments. Thus, persistence compensates for reduced energy. There is the practical need to keep energy in reserve. Discipline implies self control, courage to stop working as soon as signs of fatigue appear. In fact psychologists differentiate between *perseverance* and *perseveration*. The former means steady persistence in a course of action in spite of difficulties, obstacles, or discouragement. The latter refers to a pathological condition of continuing or repeating an action without the ability to stop or shift to more productive behavior. Fatigue or boredom should be a signal to stop working and resort to either of the two other strategies, play or leisure. Waiting for official breaks or weekend does not provide a ready solution.

WORK HABITS AND ORGANIZATION CULTURE

Work habits play a significant role in energy management. Habits develop sometimes consciously, at other times subconsciously. There will always be a measure of individual freedom and discovery of available options. However, the culture of the organization presents many obstacles. Take for example, the tradition of lengthy meetings not to mention the mismanagement of meetings. A worker rushing from one meeting to the next without transitional breaks is most damaging to mental health. Intense involvement in a meeting loads the brain with a lot of noise. This noise should be discharged from the system before the worker starts worrying about the next meeting. Hence, it is most important to avail oneself of a transitional period to get rid of after effects of one meeting and be composed enough to start participation in the next meeting or task. I advise my students to avail themselves of what I call "islands of tranquility" during the working day, such as breaks between meetings.

PSYCHOLOGY OF OVERLOAD

Sensory overload is indicated by increased incoming inputs through the senses. Sensory overload is often contiguous with over-ideation, or too many ideas, commitments and preoccupations. Thoughts are never neutral. They have the power to arouse emotions causing a lot of stress which in turn, interferes with sleep, if not with sound thinking. Over-ideation is a state of arousal which interferes with concentration, causing restlessness and random behavior. Overload may be caused by unresolved dilemmas or delayed decisions. Leisure is required to bring these forces under control. We cannot carry on striving indefinitely in doing work without clearing the system of preoccupations which are irrelevant to on-going demands of reality. That is, one function of leisure is to take time out to confront the enemies within.

FINAL CONCLUSION

I end this chapter by a reflection which has crossed my mind. Whether at work or during retirement, energy management will remain with us to the end of life. We cannot escape the responsibility for achieving balance and harmony among these three modes of existence. What is left to accomplish is a wrap up of the essential themes of this chapter which I sum up briefly in the following points:

*

Man is biologically destined to live in relation to the world — more than simply securing a place in it. He exists as an environmental force. In other words, he is destined to change the environment through work. And by changing the environment, man changes himself.

*

Two motives, or needs, are primary or intrinsic in man since infancy: *the need to know the world, and the need to achieve competence.*

*

Any skill is regulated by emotive restraint, perseverance and self control. This applies equally to intellectual skill, as well as to what might be considered essentially physical skill.

*

I think we psychologists fail to do justice to the dignity of working men and women by so much fuss about *work motivation*. It is not just work motivation. *It is natural need to thrive as an active agent in the world.*

✳

The final outcome of technology development depends to a great extent on how we manage technology and the structures of institutions built around it. Unfortunately, so far we are confronted with the bitter fact that organizational ability lags behind scientific innovation and the resulting technological advance. Lots of efforts are needed to bridge this gap.

PHILOSOPHICAL FOUNDATIONS IN QUOTES

The quotes within are statements I've made in various countries, for more than three decades. They were extracted from my teaching by my students during their participation. Somehow the statements strongly impacted the students to the extent that they cared to record them, and present them to me in writing. They were statements that I uttered spontaneously and without prior rehearsing. Some of my students humorously called them "Moneim's throwaways."

Each of these quotes is a distillation of a *lived philosophy* and deserves a chapter in a book to demonstrate its profound implications to our lives. Encouraged by the impact of these quotes on the audience, I decided to add others, extracted from my more recent lectures and seminars. Naturally, quotes reported by my audience have been edited to correct occasional errors of hearing or interpretation. All quotes in this chapter constitute fair reflection of my views in a concise and distinct way. The quotes can serve as topics for discussion and/or further elaboration by the reader.

To facilitate inspection, I classified the quotes on the basis of content. They fall into 15 categories which are presented in alphabetical order. The quotes within each category were left in random order. Below is a list of the categories as they are presented in this chapter:

- Communication
- Conflict
- Culture
- Energy
- Family
- Leading–Managing
- Membership and Roles
- Motivation
- Organizations
- Power and Influence
- Self Awareness
- Stress
- Thinking
- Time and Change
- Values

COMMUNICATION

1. One cannot *not* communicate: At least 60% of the messages people receive from you are non-verbal.

2. Shared perception is the foundation of communication: Who am I to you and who you are to me with reference to the purpose of our encounter at a particular time. We must also ensure shared understanding of the surrounding conditions.

3. Much communication is simply noise — a message must have *informative* value. Furthermore, the message which fails to trigger feedback is lost forever. A message not received as intended is futile.

4. Anger is a state of arousal, available energy associated with pain. Energy must be channeled into a forceful message to the person that aroused the anger. Unexpressed anger binds energy within. That is what might be called "impotent anger."

5. We often overlook the role of silence in communication. Listening is not easy. Like any other skill, listening can be acquired. It comes naturally if you are genuinely curious about what another party's views and feelings are.

6. Communication system in the organization is what the central nervous system is to the organism. It's the manager's job to facilitate the flow of information within his immediate unit and between his unit and other units in the organization.

7. Communication isn't just between you and others. You're communicating with yourself all the time. Self-talk is often a form of auto-hypnosis. Watch your language, particularly when talking to yourself.

8. Your voice has a significant impact on your social environment. How you talk will enhance, or detract from, your public image. In some

professions, voice is the single most important ingredient in communication.

9. In dealing with an autocratic boss… you ought to establish your presence through talking, answering questions, correcting misperception, justifying your views. Maintain the upright posture while your boss is talking. Let him or her hear his own voice. Soon, he or she will realize you are there as a person in your own right.

10. *Nagging* is a peculiar human phenomenon. It is built on prior consent between two people. They persist in talking to each other with no intent to agree. The consent is described eloquently by Eric Berne, "let you and I keep fighting." That is one of the most self-defeating human inventions.

11. Gossip in an organization moves people very quickly from collective uncertainty to collective confusion. Stop it whenever you encounter it – and for heaven's sake don't contribute to it!

12. Every society breeds its "broadcasters" — it might be useful to discover who among us is likely to play this role.

13. Gossip is a very effective communication system. It satisfies the hunger of masses for information, particularly in periods of uncertainty. Rather than alleviating uncertainty, it produces confusion due to randomness and overload.

14. Communications occur at two levels: the message itself and the "meta-message" — the intention behind the message.

15. Feedback from subordinates is important to the manager, not because of the emotional support or recognition, but because it lessens ambiguity and tension, therefore, it's like a shot of energy.

16. There is absolutely no way you can find out what goes on in the heart and mind of another human being unless that person lets you in. As Jaspers stated, "The truth begins when two people meet."

CONFLICT

17. People confuse conflict with animosity. That explains the prevalence of avoidance strategies.

18. The courage to define the boundaries of conflict is a great skill in leadership.

19. Righteous anger intensifies conflict and drives away humor.

20. Accommodation in resolving conflict isn't necessarily a reflection of weakness. It may indicate a choice from position of strength and self confidence.

21. Withdrawal in reaction to conflict dissipates your presence and weakens your membership in the group.

22. Conflict that remains underground can, in the long run, have a very destructive effect on people and organizations.

23. In group decision making, a manager must acknowledge the losing minority's authentic participation in deliberation. Recognize the legitimacy of their right to differ and give reassurance of their continued membership.

24. Conflict is natural. We should expect, and tolerate it. Our job is to manage it. In a conflict situation, the manager's first responsibility is to contain and prevent if from escalation or from spreading beyond the issues that gave rise to conflict.

25. In resolving conflict, there's no substitute for communication. It's simply talking about our different views and feelings.

26. Best way to get another person to clarify his position is to take a clear position yourself. On crucial issues, this is a moral imperative.

CULTURE

27. It took me years to realize that there must be something that transcends localities and specific cultures, since I get the same [positive] response irrespective of cultural differences. It seems that I am dealing with what is essentially human rather than what is specifically local or domestic. And I have always believed that in anthropological and sociological research, we tend to overemphasize differences between cultures and there is not enough work on commonalities.

28. I am keenly aware of similarities and differences between cultures. I come on hard on those who explain everything in cultural terms. I stress the features that are universally human. I discern characteristics which are individual from what is cultural and what is species-specific. Quite often cultural influence is used as excuse for doing what should not be done or for failing to do what should be done. I am rather daring in my critique of such tendency. My critique is usually accepted partly because people do not see me as adversary. They are well aware that I come from a developing country. By criticizing management practices in Malaysia or Singapore, for example, I am criticizing my own cultural baggage as well.

29. I think what people enjoy most [in my seminars] is that I do not cancel them out. I invite them to think with me, I start from their life conditions, their objectives, the dilemmas that they face. In fact, I call any of my seminars 'a voyage.' I enter into the classroom to invite people to go on a journey together.

30. If you don't have a role, your membership is incomplete; you are not included. A role is the vehicle for inclusion in a group/organization.

31. Personality is a set of potentialities that unfold only when we assume a role in a social system. The social role is the mechanism whereby we learn and express our potentialities.

32. The quality of membership is central in my conceptualization of human society in business or elsewhere.

ENERGY

33. Runaway phenomena — in moments of panic, people act without coherent framework.

34. Focusing your energy on the solvable problems — key to success in managing daily stress.

35. Even in receiving energy you are expending energy.

36. Judge not vitality by the amount of energy you expend, but the amount of energy you keep in store.

37. The more organized a system is, the more information it yields and the more it attains.

38. If you are a highly dedicated, energetic manager, desiring to act and you're dealing with people less dedicated and with less energy, who is going to lose energy to whom?

39. The minute you start an organization, it starts to run down. Do not ignore the law of entropy.

40. Intervention by the manager doesn't guarantee energy increase. Your excess energy can drain others, and may cause randomness. Your intervention has to be calculated.

41. *Restoring order* takes more energy than the energy expended in *creating order*. That is the wisdom of the statement, "Prevention is better than cure."

42. Boundary activity is really a process of importation and exportation of energy.

43. Waste is disintegrated energy. Pollution is just another name for entropy. Gossip and rumor are manifestations of social pollution.

44. Boredom is a form of static equilibrium, absence of stimulation, apathy, the end result of the entropic process.

45. Don't take sanity for granted. Monitor your energy every minute of the day — we need *islands of tranquility* during the working day, even few minutes of rest every once in a while. Don't wait for the weekends.

FAMILY

46. The more we live together, the more prejudiced we become. Relationships have to be nursed.

47. Parenting is divisive if it always deals with children one-to-one. Parents need to see the family as a whole unit.

48. It takes between 5 to 8 years to be a competent plumber. How many does it take before we become effective husbands, wives, or parents? We have no training in these vital matters.

49. Marriage is linking of two sub-systems.

50. Marriage is not a finished state: "I love you, you love me, we get married, that is it." We get married, we move to a new level of existence, very challenging and very demanding. We get married, we rise beyond individuality, and we enter an association. We accept membership in a new social structure which has to be our creation together.

51. Some parents with good intentions actually prevent the sense of the whole family from emerging because of their style of communications, one-to-one with each member.

LEADING-MANAGING

52. You cannot *"not* manage."

53. Leading starts in the mind.

54. Leadership is not something within you. It is what goes on between you and others.

55. Leading is an encounter involving two parties in a process of reciprocal activation.

56. Management is the art of relevance.

57. Management is the art of talking with the intent to influence.

58. You seldom manage separate individuals. More often than not, you manage groups, i.e.; social structures. You can't use principles of intrapersonal psychology to manage a group. Leading a group requires dramatic shift in perspective.

59. Managing a group is like surfing, or navigating. You ride waves of interactions, exchanges, crises, and a turbulent environment.

60. Your image in the organization is enhanced if you engage in meaningful activities beyond the boundary of your immediate unit. Establishing your presence in the organization reinforces your authority among both your peers and subordinates.

61. The primary objective of a new manager should be to become a member as quickly as possible, to be included. Don't try to prove you're better than your predecessor. Let the group that you have just joined discover that through your conduct and decisions.

62. As you move to a new position, don't assume that your success in the past can be extrapolated into the new situation.

63. Your problem starts, not ends, with hiring an expert.

64. The manager is, by definition, a *boundary* figure. He or she is the only person in a group who has the ultimate responsibility for managing the interface between the group and other groups.

65. If everybody is very busy doing a good job, who is taking care of the organization as a whole?

66. The manager's job is like that of the orchestra director who orchestrates many instruments without necessarily playing a single instrument.

67. If you chose the autocratic approach, you must expect to encounter opposition sooner or later. You'd better develop a thick skin.

68. Manager has to fight the *illusion of helplessness* in subordinates, and probably in him/ her. Why do we treat our subordinates as mentally bankrupt?

69. Human beings dislike disorder. Your subordinates will respect you to the extent that you are able to provide order.

70. A question I always pose to managers in my classes, "where do you position yourself in the organization as a whole system?"

71. Differentiation through specialization strains integration. Hiring the best minds is not enough — the challenge is to assimilate and integrate these people into the total system we call "organization."

72. Delegation isn't giving up authority; it's activating the potentialities of subordinates.

73. By inviting very creative people to join the organization, you are in effect importing problems — many creative people are ruthlessly autocratic and independent. Creativity is potential energy that has to be managed; it isn't the *final* solution to the problem.

74. Leadership minus membership spells disaster.

75. When charisma excludes our ability to criticize, and see, the human realities of the leader, that he is different from God, then we have a dangerous situation — people would not be relating to a real person in flesh and blood who can go wrong some of the time.

76. I, as a leader, should be considered useless without the contributions of my subordinates and it is the duty of my subordinates to complement me, rather than put so much faith in me and leave me alone and say 'you are God, we are here to follow you.'

77. A leader must be similar enough to be understood and yet, different enough to justify his or her authority.

78. Leadership may well be defined as a stream of energy that flows back and forth between a leader and followers. It is a process of mutual activation.

79. I define *Followership* as the leader's readiness to put dominance on hold and assume a receptive posture that allows him to acquire necessary information. How else could he make use of expert resources?

80. Obedience is the worst form of relating to a leader.

81. Leading people is a very serious affair, even dangerous sometimes. You have no idea how much people can suffer from even well-intentioned but ineffective leadership.

82. To understand leadership, we need to see the followership dimension as well. A leader who is totally a leader presents a distorted picture. You're not a leader until your authority is legitimated by followers.

83. Very few leaders have *the will to lead* free of a measure of ambivalence. Besides, the will to lead is a relative motivational force. But you as a leader must have enough of it to be able to mobilize personality resources in yourself as well as in others.

84. In my view a leader must actualize the leadership potentialities inherent in the group. Only then, leadership becomes a pervasive social phenomenon.

85. I receive more complaints from subordinates about hesitant leadership than autocratic leadership. People want order, structure, and clear direction.

86. Many people don't care less about assuming a leadership role. They care much about having influence, and significant role in the system.

87. It is a false dichotomy to divide people into only two categories — leaders and followers, one category for the fortunate and another category for the mentally bankrupt.

88. "Lead, follow, or get out of the way!" — There isn't a human being on earth who is exclusively a leader or exclusively a follower. But we all need exchange of influence.

89. Leadership doesn't start in action — it starts in perception.

90. You can never be a leader until you've been included into, and accepted by, a group.

91. You cannot expect people to be excited by your vision if you don't communicate it. You also need to be clear about how people will fit into your vision and the context within which you will implement your vision.

92. If you get total obedience from your subordinates, you have already been cancelled out as a leader... subordinates will defeat your leadership by passively waiting for your next directive.

93. Never let anybody you are leading become a total follower. Passive obedience is the most destructive mode of relating to a boss.

94. Some models of leadership are derived from the drill sergeant or macho mentality.

95. It is the responsibility of the leader to activate the leadership capacities in those around him. A repressive leader is really depriving himself of needed resources around him...

96. In this age of information systems and chronic information overload, the capacity to select the most relevant information for decision making will be the most critical requirement for effective leadership.

97. According to the Japanese, you don't have to be the most intelligent or the strongest to lead. More importantly, you must be respected, endowed with *moral authority* and wisdom developed over a long time.

98. Your style of leadership is in essence, your style of communication.

99. Leadership potential isn't enough to rise; it needs to be mediated by *followership*. Paradoxical, isn't it?

100. Top leadership of a large organization requires a higher level of conceptualization than leadership at the middle or lower levels.

101. Organizational dynamics are very different from group dynamics. Success as a "team leader" does not guarantee success at the organizational level. Many executives do not yet understand the shift required.

102. A meeting that ends without clear outcome must have started without clarity, especially in the leader's mind — unless he or she was acting deliberately to manipulate people.

103. Top leadership requires strategic thinking involving abstraction, formulating models, synthesis — and imagination. However, strategic thinking must be supported by sensitivity to details and how the details fit into a general pattern.

104. Leadership is a network of relationships, not an intrapersonal phenomenon. It has to be understood within a social context that determines the type of leadership, etc.

105. I regret the fact that leadership is no more a natural phenomenon to be observed where it takes place in society. It became what we study in management development programs or institutions of public administration.

106. The skills of integration are strictly managerial, not technical.

107. Clients can serve as an integration force if service is the common culture of different departments of the same institution.

108. Integration is the process or mechanisms or procedures which preserve the wholeness of the system.

109. No organization should differentiate before it is ready to integrate.

110. Many organizations just do not know how to effectively integrate themselves despite good intentions and high level of technical competency.

111. Integration is not an ideal, but a matter of necessary strategy. However, integration mechanisms should not wipe out diversity.

112. Your clients are not just consumers, they are sources of innovation. They can help you improve existing products or service, or create new products and services.

113. As you shift from one managerial style to another, you're really only shifting from one mode of communication to another. Managerial style is essentially a communication style.

114. You should never act out of character. Take charge in your own way. Your model of leadership should derive from your own experience. Discover your own resources.

115. Ineffective use of a particular managerial style usually results from: (a) acting out of character; (b) overuse; (c) absence of skill in the use of that style; or (d) misreading the fields of your action.

116. A very significant flaw in managers is unbridled readiness to act, to intervene. That type of manager will never rise beyond the middle level because they cannot tolerate uncertainty.

117. Delegation is the key to the developer style. It requires awareness of the potential of people. You also must demonstrate, and update, your expertise. Expertise enhances your legal authority.

118. In managing a team of specialists you need skills in working with group dynamics. You also have to develop skills in talking to a group, which is different from talking to individuals.

119. I prefer the expression, *corrective information* than *negative feedback*. Corrective information is invaluable service you provide to people to make sure that they are in touch with reality since they carry the burden of living in it.

120. A system does not survive by congratulation notes. It survives as long as it remains a learning system.

MEMBERSHIP AND ROLES

121. It is wrong to say that individuals exist *in* — meaning *inside* — the organization. The organization, or any social system, is not a *container* for individuals. A social system *emerges* as a result of people willing to live in relation to each other in a collectivity that transcends their respective individualities. *Membership* is the proper definition of our social existence. We *exist in relation to* — rather than *inside* the organization. We assume interdependent roles that make up the organization.

122. Regardless of how objectionable we may find some people, we should recognize the legitimacy in their position; there is always sense in other people's behavior whether we see it or not.

123. Why do we insist that people be like mathematical equations — balanced and symmetrical. Contradictions are inherent in every human being. Each individual is an entire universe, whole and complex.

124. A business person is not exclusively a business person. Successful entrepreneurs rarely think about the outcome [of their labor] in terms of dollars. They are fascinated by the process itself, and that is why they may get bankrupt but rise again. What is really most exciting in business is problem solving, decision making, struggling with odds, seeing more possibilities. A person who is hung up on the dollar I don't think can make a good banker or a good entrepreneur at all.

125. Role clarity is a reciprocal process.

126. Influence is a duty which accompanies real membership.

127. Role is the mediator between external behavior and internal structure. If you want to really understand a person, see how his role, his natural role, evolves spontaneously over time.

128. No one can be totally included in a single social system, whether it were a firm or university or even a family. Each one of us belongs to several social systems at the same time. And unless you reach for the whole person beyond any single membership, you cannot function well anywhere.

129. Often, managers participating in my seminars around the world refer to what they call the phenomenon of deadwood. I always tell them "no human being can be deadwood." A human being can only be a parasite. And a parasite can control the entire organism. Any person without a role can spread chaos — intentionally or unintentionally. A role properly defined is the only way we can prevent people from leading a parasitic existence.

130. It is your responsibility to define your own role in relation to other roles. There are no separate roles; roles exist as a set.

131. Leadership is a social phenomenon... can only be understood within the context of interdependent roles that we call role sets... there is no escape from interdependence.

132. Role overload is a continuing danger arising from lean staffing.

133. Every member of any group, by virtue of his inclusion, carries the burden of influencing the group. Influence isn't a luxury but a responsibility.

134. If you are aware of the group, as a group, as entity to be managed, then you must know the role(s) individuals assume in the group. They are not just individuals but members of a social system. As a leader, you must recognize this context of group dynamics and even help others to have a role, to have presence in the group.

135. A role is a social concept, a set of relationships. A role never exists except relative to another role. A manager therefore must provide clarity about roles and recognize interdependence as a fact of life.

136. When people accept your role, it becomes institutionalized. Take advantage of ambiguities that exist by defining your role in your behavior, especially if it doesn't violate organizational norms. However, do it quietly and gently and communicate it in case of resistance. All organizations are pragmatic and they will accept your redefined or new role, even reward it, if it leads to something productive.

137. Role is the conduit of your effectiveness. Manage it well. By assuming a role you are, by definition, influencing your environment or the group in a certain way.

138. Every role has a moral lining.

MOTIVATION

139. The direction of influence isn't always from boss to subordinate, but from subordinate to boss as well. Likewise, motivation is a form of energy that flows from students to a teacher or from a client to a sales person or from a patient to a doctor...

140. Without reciprocity, there will be no motivation. Reciprocity guarantees shared membership. Reciprocity connects employees and the organization.

141. Work motivation is the willingness to do what you do without feelings of sacrifice.

142. Work gives you a feeling of *becoming*, on-going process, unfolding of potentialities.

143. We need a management philosophy that recognizes people as members, as contributors, not just as followers or *subordinates*.

144. Human beings seek to inject meaningfulness in all what they do. Even people performing work at the lowest level of activities need to have a sense of *meaningfulness* in their work.

145. I dislike the word "workaholic." It implies some kind of insult. I see nothing wrong with carrying work at home as long as it is interesting and fulfilling. Separation between time for work and time for leisure is a cultural artifact. It does not exist in all cultures.

146. Any living system is in essence an *energy system* constantly transforming energy, expending and importing energy...

147. When we talk about motivation, we must first consider energy. Motivation is willingness to transform available energy into work. Work itself is a process of transforming something into something else...

148. Discipline and structure at work should be organizing and energizing, therefore productive and inventive.

149. A sizeable proportion of the so-called "un-motivated" employees have never had the opportunity to reach the level of competence that allows them the opportunity to enjoy the work assigned to them. Often, they are forced to cover up their incompetence.

150. The most potent source of motivation available to any individual is his/her self-definition. All the energy in the world is useless until you define yourself in the light of your values. Self concept is a force, not an abstract idea.

151. Motivation is often a function of traveling, commuting between two different worlds, family and work. Often, the deterioration in work productivity is related to family situations.

152. An executive once told me, "We have lost so many people who are still with us." And by the way, that executive's company had the benefit of a reputable leadership training program. Side observation: the word *supervision* did not feature anywhere in the program.

153. "How can I motivate my employees?" A question I often get from managers. My answer is usually, "You cannot." A person is not a rat in a Skinner's box. I have strong reasons for my typical answer: First, the question ignores reciprocity as fact in human relations. Second, the job of the manager is to create situations and jobs which help people discover and express their potential; providing the necessary resources and demanding that the staff take advantage of them. Motivation is not an inventory of techniques, nor is it a potion you *inject into* someone else.

154. If work is perceived as selling your labor to the employer, joy and *meaningfulness* will go out of the window, and motivation along with them.

155. Apprenticeship — a lost art in learning a job.

156. When you wake up in the morning, do you look forward to a working day? That's the real key to motivation.

157. In order to be motivated by any goal, the goal has to be perceived as *achievable*.

158. Motivation as lived experience means the willingness to mobilize as much available energy as possible in the pursuit of shared goals and common enterprise. Spontaneity is the core of work motivation.

159. A young manager once told me, "If by the end of a working day, I do not feel exhausted, I know that I did not do a good job." Poor fellow, he did not know that he was *driven*. *Driving* is the issue.

ORGANIZATIONS

160. An organization is a contrived social system. It is an artificial collectivity. We were not born into a corporation — there lies both its power and its weakness. We don't have natural instincts or traditional wisdom to help us relate to the organization as we do in the family. There is no continuity in our lives from membership in the family to membership in a corporation. However, certain cultures prepare the individual to be ready to move smoothly from family membership to membership in other societal structures. The Japanese culture allows the individual to move smoothly from the family to a school or to a corporation simply because cultural traditions and customs pervade what is personal and what is formal. The Japanese avoid the culture shock.

161. The organization has no memory. It needs a record of information from many people to remain in history and to project itself into the future.

162. There is no traditional wisdom that has been handed down to us to help us to adjust to life in a business organization. The degree of ambiguity is much greater than in any other social system known to man.

163. Identification with a job is one thing. Identification with the company is something else. They may coincide but not to the same degree.

164. Usually organizational structure lags behind strategy, but it should be close behind. Structure should support a clear-cut strategy, not vice versa.

165. The organization is more than an economic production system. It is also a legal system, a learning system, an information system, a communication system, and don't ever forget, a *social* system — connecting together many constituencies, internal and external.

166. You cannot take a photograph of an organization. When a car stops functioning, what happens to the car? It remains there. You find difficulty getting rid of it. What happens to an organization when it stops functioning? It vanishes but people just disperse.

167. Changing the image of the organization can amount to a breach of the unwritten psychological contract between members and the organization.

168. Nobody exists in the organization like a fish in a bowl. Inclusion is psychological more than physical.

169. The cutting edge of competition in the market of the future isn't purely technical innovation, but creatively finding ways to solicit and process information from clients into productive and timely responses.

170. The environment literally invades your organization every day. It is in the organization.

171. Certain degree of *decentralization* is life-saving for the organization as a whole. Decentralization allows the organization to respond quickly to changes in the environmental context. Decentralized sub-systems are the equivalent of reflex systems in the organism. Therefore, peripheral systems must be invested with some power and autonomy.

172. The organization is always in a state of flux: it grows, expands, declines, recovers or may even dissolve.

POWER AND INFLUENCE

173. As a leader, you have available to you much more than vested power, legitimate and coercive. Other sources of power will naturally accrue to you if you allow communications and influence to flow freely back and forth between you and others.

174. Power in itself does not corrupt. What corrupts is loss of membership. Leadership minus membership spells disaster.

175. The "Illusion of Helplessness" is rampant in organizations. Once you acquire power, others may stand by and watch you, keeping a balance sheet of credits and liabilities, "you're the boss, tell me what to do."

176. Punishment should be appropriate to that single act, not generalized beyond a single incident of wrongdoing...

177. Once you have established a reward and punishment system, it ceases to be motivating. Rather, it becomes a necessary condition, an expected outcome.

178. Reward is more effective in changing behavior than punishment. This is because punishment fixes attention on the wrong act, while reward emphasizes and reinforces a desirable option.

179. When you use coercion, be prepared for the consequences — withdrawal (physical or psychological), or retaliation.

180. He who defines the issues has the power.

181. The legitimate power of the manager is only the entry power; you're never totally included unless you utilize other sources of power — expert or moral.

182. Managers need as much "fellowship" as "leadership" skills, namely the ability to influence people at your level of authority, both in your organization or any other organization. That is what I like to call, *representational power* — expansion of the scope of your influence beyond immediate subordinates.

183. Humiliation is more damaging than the worst physical pain. Punishment should never violate a person's self-esteem.

184. Anybody who screens your input has power over you, as does anybody who controls your output.

185. The use of coercive power indicates bankruptcy — it should be the last resort.

186. Leadership takes place in the mind. It is not like in playing billiards: you hold a stick, push a ball and the ball hits another ball which proceeds to a hole. Leading is not pulling, it is not mechanical attraction. It is an encounter involving two parties in a process of reciprocal activation.

187. In the long run people resent deceptive appraisal because they want to grow and they want to be on firm grounds. They hate uncertainty, particularly about who they are.

SELF AWARENESS

188. Awareness of our *emotional reactions* is "the royal road to global self awareness."

189. Self-awareness depends primarily on your ability to describe your emotional reactions in specific and concrete terms. This is not as easy as it appears. It is a skill that requires practice and honesty with oneself.

190. The thermometer is one of the greatest inventions in the medical field. This simple device enables us to monitor and regulate fluctuations in our body temperature. The value of the invention lies in its simplicity. It does not require medical expertise to use it. We need similar instruments in the psychological field.

191. Anger is a painful state of mind. Suppressing anger does not put an end to the pain. Nor does it help maintain interpersonal relationships. Instead, it will generate internal tension that could build up until it becomes unbearable. The time will come when it explodes. Your conduct then would appear strange or incomprehensible.

192. I fear that psychology has been sucked into physical science. Mine is a *psychological* psychology of the human person.

193. I regret the absence of the word "sentiment" from textbooks of psychology.

194. The courage to say, "I don't know" — the first step in dealing with uncertainty, to recognize your own uncertainty.

195. Don't act out of character but correct misperceptions by increasing communications. You carry the burden of correcting your public image.

196. In judging a person, it is important to identify your immediate, instinctive, and spontaneous reaction to that person. Own up to your feelings.

197. Truth in human relationships is different from truth in science. Truth that binds us together is what you and I accept. Shared perception and authenticity are prerequisites for lasting relationships.

198. There is a difference between knowing and understanding.

199. A person may come to you for advice. Every time you offer advice, all you get from him is, "Yes, but." I made a rule in my life to stop talking after the fourth "yes, but." There are variations on "yes, but" — "I tried it but it did not work" or "on the other hand," or "what if?"

200. In my life I met two types of people: those who are so firmly grounded in their unhappiness. They defend their right for their grievances and expect you to endorse their reasons. Fortunately, I met others who have strong reasons to complain and be unhappy. And yet, they somehow consider their misfortunes to be natural events for which nobody is to blame. To the latter type, misfortunes do not define life as a whole. They do not allow their misfortunes to cloud their judgment or disturb their relations with other people. Their endurance brings them closer to people and raise their standing in the eyes of others. They do not see themselves as victims. They continue to consider life worth living despite their suffering. Indeed, happiness can be a choice and misery can become a career.

201. There is much talk about the value of "self awareness" yet we rarely state what we mean by "self." As it is not possible to gain awareness of the "self" in its entirety, it would be wise to aim at becoming aware of something specific. The important thing to do is develop a habit of focusing attention on what happens to us all the time as life goes on.

202. Our sensory apparatus is built-in communication system. It connects us all the time to events that occur around us or in our own bodies, whereas our emotional reactions are statements about how the world impacts us at a given moment in time. Sensitivity to both sensations and emotions are the core of what we call self awareness.

203. Personality is not a fixed entity, it is not a finished product at any time, it is a continuous process of *becoming*.

204. Personality is a set of potentialities that unfold only when we assume a role in a social system. The social role is the mechanism whereby we learn and express our potentialities.

205. I do not think that life is a rose garden. But I think that life *is*. I like a remark made by Madame Curie: "life is not to be feared. It's simply to be understood." And when you understand it, you can put up with it.

206. Meaningfulness in life comes as a result of what we do, from engaging in activities of worth to us, and not from introspection.

207. Best way to be objective is to recognize your emotions, feelings, not to avoid or deny them.

208. The only way you can achieve anything is to convince yourself that you can live without it.

209. I think it would be a great loss if you teach what I teach, because every human being has something to offer, and has to reach for what is unique in himself or herself. So you could be inspired by me, and I could be inspired by you.

STRESS

210. Neutralization — the realization that sources of stress occur outside in the world about you, not *inside* you.

211. There are people who can actually be noxious to your well-being. Recognize them and avoid them as much as possible.

212. Major stressors or disasters are limited in one's life history. It is the common daily pressures that break our backs after a while.

213. Over-active managers engage more in *busy-ness* than real *business*... There is a difference between agitation and vitality.

214. If a person is angry at you, listen first and talk later. Anger is a significant source of vital information.

215. When you are angry, you should recognize that anger is something that is happening to you — it is *not* you, you are not the anger. We need to learn how to *dis-identify* with negative events happening to us. Separate yourself as a whole person from what is happening to you.

216. It takes over 1000 muscles for a human being to maintain the upright posture, to counteract the pull of gravity. Depression reduces resistance to the pull of gravity.

217. Gross physical activity is one of the best remedies to counteract the tyranny of the mind.

218. You are the sole navigator of your own life.

219. The intensity of family experience is transferred to the job when you identify too strongly with it. Much conflict stems from over-identification which means over-personalization of relationships.

220. In a complex social setting like a corporation, we all need a support system. This need is much greater than in the past: since the weakening of a sense of community. The extended family has been weakened. Even the nuclear family is breaking down.

221. Emotions vs. feelings... many people confuse them. Emotions are spontaneous, momentary expressions, like anger; feelings are more enduring. I can be extremely angry at you and yet remain very close to you in bond. Feelings are organized emotions relating to another person, a place or a thing.

222. Feelings are not *irrational*. They are *a-rational*, that is to say, they pertain to a different mode of existence in relation to the world.

223. Often in the course of living I have discovered solutions to serious problems when I have stopped trying to seek them. We are much more creative when we relax, and stop pushing.

THINKING

224. It is odd that we tend to talk about creativity before we understand the intricacies of ordinary thinking.

225. Thinking is intrinsically a social process, even when we talk to ourselves.

226. Socrates made it his business to challenge sophists in the streets of Athens: posing questions and refraining from giving answers. Plato did not write books. He simply recorded dialogues of Socrates with his disciples. Socrates dared people to think. And for that, he paid his life. It is said that the death of Socrates marks the beginning of philosophy.

227. Clarity gives you an air of forcefulness, even if it were clarity about being unclear.

228. Clutter is the antidote of clarity.

229. Learning isn't just a process of knowledge acquisition. It includes a process of forgetting — excluding what is irrelevant and synthesizing what is relevant to the person as a whole entity.

230. We need a telescope as well as a microscope to understand complex problems. Strategic thinking is telescopic. Close observation of reality is microscopic. They alternate and complement one another... zooming is the issue.

231. Imaginativeness is a significant factor in problem-solving and in maintaining human relationships.

232. "I wonder" attitude is antidote to prejudice, and the beginning of a dialogue.

233. "Single-cause" thinking leads to piecemeal decisions, putting out fires, and incremental management.

234. Perception is always selective. Reality presents itself to us and we select what seems most important to us.

235. Risk is not the same thing as uncertainty. With risk you have at least some information and you fill in the gaps through inference, or probability. In the case of uncertainty there is absence of information, void, and randomness.

236. Without theory, you don't see enough of reality. A good theory or model actually brings you closer to reality by keeping you from dismissing relevant information and helping you to dismiss the irrelevant.

237. You cannot rise in an organization beyond the limits of your perception.

238. Common sense is stored lived experience.

239. Imagination is the mental extension of sensory experience.

240. The human brain does not tolerate disorder, or randomness. A turbulent environment is perceived by us as random, lacking order and predictability. We seek structure to reduce randomness; that's why we invent theoretical models to guide our steps in a complex and turbulent world.

241. Management is the art of relevance. It takes effort to focus on what is relevant.

242. The most creative activity is primarily *looking* to *see* clearly, and pausing to *hear* distinctly.

243. Clarity clears the way for action. It is a liberating force.

244. In an encounter with another person, clarity about what you stand for forces the other person to define his or her position. Clarity then becomes the basis for authenticity in human relationships.

245. Lack of knowledge isn't the only source of uncertainty; too much information will also increase uncertainty. *Relevant* information is what we need.

246. Many managers are propelled to act — they conclude too early. Others are over-ideational — as a result they miss opportunities for timely action.

247. There is no such thing as "reality as it is." Reality is what you perceive it to be — how you interpret it to yourself. You need other observers. Shared perception may save your life.

248. Subjectivity is the conduit to objective thinking. Recognize your biases.

249. Originality of the ordinary: The genius of Newton lies in the fact that he was able to wonder about what is most obvious — "why do things fall down rather than hang in the air?"

250. There's nothing more practical than a good theory.

251. Clarity is not commensurate to the volume of knowledge... what is really needed is relevant information.

252. Hard decisions shouldn't be made when you're bored, tired, or overactive.

253. When a genius makes a mistake, usually the mistake has disastrous consequences. Only a highly intelligent person can steal a bank, or carry out a major scam, or swindles a community of investors or launches a war against a weak nation.

254. Un-communicated ideas quickly fade away.

255. Intelligence is a tool that may be used, over-used, abused, or misused.

256. Changing a state of uncertainty into a risk-taking situation implies denial of uncertainty.

257. You don't really choose solutions, but only new problems which you can cope with.

258. A problem becomes a problem when you define it as such and stay there. A problem is an invitation to action. It follows that you must move from being problem-centered to solution bound. Otherwise you become part of the problem.

259. It is very dangerous to accept someone else's definition of a problem when you are the person who is supposed to solve it.

260. A wise manager once told me: "The problem I am confronted with is much too important a matter to be left to my boss."

261. My mission as a teacher is not to provide a forum where participants learn from each other, but to unlearn much of what they have learned over the years. This is particularly crucial when the students are intelligent adults whose learning of management has been faulty. My mission is to get participants learn from *me*. I provide a forum where they confront the faulty assumptions that cloud their thinking. My teaching would be worthless if I failed to clear their minds from slogans and semi-scientific rubbish.

262. Sociability corrupts if it were not guided by clarity of purpose and sincere intention to *rethink*.

263. Learning is not a process of amassing disparate bits of information but extracting the essential lessons in the light of our values and goals. In learning, we must exercise what I like to call *cognitive assertiveness*.

TIME AND CHANGE

264. There is no such thing as "the future." There are many possible futures. You have to decide what future you want for yourself or for your organization. You choose the future that you need and deserve.

265. Personality is never a finished product. It is a set of potentialities that unfold in time in response to certain circumstances.

266. The journey is as important as the destination. If you don't reach the destination, remember that you enjoyed the journey.

267. *The past is* gone forever, it is irretrievable. We have only two choices: to capture grounds lost or gain new grounds.

268. The most important person in my life is the person I choose to be with at a given moment in time.

269. People abhor boredom. They need change and the expectation of change that is seen as rational. People reject violently any change that hasn't been explained but many leaders see this as rejection of change.

270. In times of turbulent change, members of an organization think and worry separately. They may have no opportunity to exchange their concerns and fears. When they meet on occasions, they derive a great deal of comfort from the discovery that their colleagues share the same concerns and suffer similar ambiguities. Getting clearer together has the effect of magic on morale. I want every member after each encounter to say to himself or herself: "Yes, these are hard times, but we are still there, and together. Changes may be *happening* around us but we are determining our own change to continue as a thriving organization. We are *in charge* of our change."

VALUES

271. Employee hiring practices seem to value homogeneity more than diversity, conformity more than originality. And yet HR specialists claim that they value creativity. Organizations are well-advised to re-examine their criteria of selection.

272. Whatever virtue you see in personality implies hazards under certain circumstances. Therefore, look for offsetting characteristics.

273. The value system functions like a gyroscope, or regulating mechanism within you to ensure a measure of continuity and consistency.

274. Your value system is your "life policy."

275. Each virtue carries with it a liability or blind spot. Virtue, by definition, grows from an excess, giving rise to negative side-effects.

276. Some observed deficiencies in people may be negative side-effects of highly valued assets or virtues.

277. People come in packages: In selection of people (same holds true in marriage) try to take people as a "package deal" with both desirable and less desirable features. What you really should be choosing are the defects you're willing to tolerate because they go in tandem with the virtues you value most. Otherwise, you would commit the error of over-generalizing either positively or negatively from a single feature — the "halo effect" as psychologists call them.

278. Why is it that in hiring people we look for leadership qualities when, in fact, these people won't assume leadership for 5–10 years?

279. It is very well that we increase our fortunes and the fortunes of our clients, but we must do that in a manner that impresses young people. There must be elegance, there must be ethics, there must be originality. I hope that every organization becomes a social institution, a respectable institution, an inspiring institution.

280. Some people have the compulsion to see defects in others — their perception is equivalent to psychological graffiti.

281. The most important thing I learnt from my teaching experience is that once I saw sense in what I said, I tell myself afterwards: "If this is what you really think, why don't act accordingly?" Thus, the advice I offer becomes almost like a sort of public commitment, commitment to follow what I say, to practice what I preach. So many of the things I mention in my class as ideals that people can live up to, became realities in my life.

References

✳

Allport, G. W. (1983). *Becoming: Basic Considerations for a Psychology of Becoming*. New Haven: Yale University Press.

Allport, G. W. (1954). *The Nature of Prejudice*. Cambridge, MA: Adison-Wesley.

Angier, N. (1991, 30 July). As busy as a bee. *The New York Times*.

Ardrey, R. (1966). *The Territorial Imperative: A Personal Inquiry into the Animal Origins of Property and Nations*. New York: Dell Publishing Co.

Arendt, H. (1958). *The Human Condition*. Chicago: The University of Chicago Press.

Aristotle (1992). *The Politics*. (transl. T. A. Sinclair). New York: Penguin Books. 455–457.

Arrow, K. J. (1974). *The Limits of Organization*. New York: W. W. Norton.

Bart, P. (1971). The myth of a value free psychiatry. In W. Bell and J. Mau (Eds.), *The Sociology of the Future*. New York: Russell Sage Foundation.

Bellak, L. (1970). *The Porcupine Dilemma: Reflections on the Human*

Condition. New York: Citadel Press.

Bennett, S. (2007/2008). Crazy talk: Revisiting postman and the relational dynamics of communicating through personal mobile media. In *General Semantics Bulletin*. Vol. 74 / 75. 112–124.

Berger, P. L. (1963). *Invitation to Sociology: A Humanistic Perspective*. Garden City, NY: Doubleday & Co.

Berger, P., & Luckmann, T. (1966). *The Social Construction of Reality*. Garden City, N.Y.: Anchor Books.

Berger, P., Berger, B., & Kellner, H. (1973). *The Homeless Mind: Modernization and Consciousness*. New York: Random House.

Bergson, H. (1998). *The Creative Evolution* (transl. A. Mitchell). Mineola, New York: Dover publications (first published 1911).

Berloff, R. O. (Eds.) (1989). *Psychology and Work: Productivity, Change, and Employment*. Washington, D. C.: American Psychological Association.

Berne, E. (1966). *The Structure and Dynamics of Organizations and Groups*. New York: Grove Press.

Berry, J. W., Kim, U., Power, S., Young, M. & Bujaki, M. (1989). Acculturation attitudes in plural societies. *Applied Psychology: An International Review*. 38 (2) 185-206.

Brown, J. A. C. (1972). *The Social Psychology of Industry*. Middlesex, UK: Penguin Books (first published 1954).

Castaneda, C. (1974). *Journey to Ixtlan: The Lessons of Don Juan*. New York: Pocket Books.

Cattell, H. B. (1989). *Personality in Depth*. Champaign, IL.: Institute of Personality and Ability Testing.

Chemers, M. M., & Ayman, R. (Eds.) (1993). *Leadership, Theory and Research: Perspectives and Directions*. New York: Academic Press.

Colman, Arthur D. & Bexton, W. Harold (Eds.). (1975). *Group Relations Reader*. San Rafael, California: Grex Russell.

Cox, T., & Blake, S. (1991). Managing for cultural diversity: Implications for organizational effectiveness. *Academy of Management Executive. 5*, 45–56.

Dewey, J. (1954). *The Public and Its Problems*. Chicago: The Swallow Press.

El-Meligi, A. M. (1954). An Experimental Investigation of Some Aspects of "Psychological Ability" and Their Relationship with Neuroticism. Unpublished Ph.D. Thesis; Senate House Library, London University.

El-Meligi, A. M. (1968). Hallucinatory experience as a dialogue with reality. *Contemporary Psychology*. Vol. 13, No. 4, 198–200.

El-Meligi, A. M. (1977) (with Surkis). The scientific study of inner experience: a general systems approach. *The Journal of Orthomolecular Psychiatry*. Vol. 6, 3.

El-Meligi, A. M. (2002). The Environment: Humanizing & Dehumanizing Conditions. Paper presented at the meetings of the *Egyptian American Association of Scholars*. In The Library of Alexandria, Alexandria, Egypt. December 28–30, 2002.

Fleishman, E. A., & Zaccaro, S. J. (1992). Toward a taxonomy of team performance functions. In R. W. Sweezy & E. Salas (Eds.). *Teams: Their Training and Performance*. (pp. 31–56). Norwood, NJ: Ablex.

Freilich, M. (1964, August). The natural triad in kinship and complex systems. [Extract from an edited book] *American Sociological Review*. Vol. 29, No. 4.

Gibson, J. J. (1979). *The Ecological Approach to Visual Perception*. Boston: Houghton Mifflin. Reprinted 1986, Erlbaum.

Gibson, E. J. (1988). Exploratory behavior in the development of perceiving, acting, and the acquiring of knowledge. *Ann. Rev. Psychol.* 39:1–41.

Greeno, J. G. (1994). Gibson Affordances. *Psychological Review*. Vol. 101, No. 2, 336–342.

Hackman, J. R. (Ed.). (1990). *Groups That Work and Those That Don't: Creating Conditions for Effective Teamwork*. San Francisco: Jossey-Bass.

Heider, F. (1959). *The Psychology of Interpersonal Relations*. New York: John Wiley & Sons.

Heiss, J. S. (1963). The dyad views the newcomer. *Human Relations*. Vol. 16, No. 3, 241–248.

Hills, J., Le Grand, J., & Piachaud, D. (Eds.). (2002). *Understanding Social Exclusion*. Oxford: Oxford University Press.

Hobson, J. M. (2004). *The Eastern Origin of Western Civilization*. New York: Cambridge University Press.

Hoffman, L. W. (1986). Work, family, and the child. In M. S. Pallak & R. O. Perloff (Eds.), *Psychology and Work: Productivity, Change, and Employment* (pp. 173–220). Washington, DC: American Psychological Association.

Ilgen, D. R. (1999). Teams embedded in organizations. *American Psychologist*. 129–139.

Koffka, K. (1935). *Principles of Gestalt Psychology*. New York: Harcourt, Brace & Company.

Korzybski, A. (1974). *Manhood of Humanity* (first published 1931), pp. 9–111 and 186.

Kraus, E. M. (1998). *The Metaphysics of Experience: A Companion to Whitehead's Process and Reality*. New York: Fordham University Press.

Labich, K. (1990). Elite teams get the job done. *Fortune*. February 19, 90–99.

Lamont, M. (2000). *The Dignity of Working Men: Morality and the*

Boundaries of Race, Class, and Immigration. Cambridge, Mass.: Harvard University Press.

Loizos, P. (1980). Images of man. In J. Cherfas, & R. Lewin, (Eds.) *Not Work Alone: A Cross-Cultural View of Activities Superfluous to Survival*. Beverly Hills, California: Sage Publications. 231–247.

MacGrath, J. E., & Grunefeld, D. H. (1993). Toward a dynamic and systemic theory of groups: An integration of six temporally enriched perspectives. In Chemers, M. M., & Ayman, R. (Eds.). *Leadership, Theory and Research: Perspectives and Directions*. New York: Academic Press. 217–243.

MacNeal, E. (2003). *ETC: A Review of General Semantics*. 124–137.

Mai-Dalton, R. R. (1993). Managing diversity on the individual, group, and organizational levels. In M. M. Chemers, & R. Ayman (Eds). *Leadership, Theory and Research: Perspectives and Directions*. New York: Academic Press. 189–215.

McCaskey, M. B., Athos, A. G., & Barrett, D. (1979). *Framework for Analyzing Work Groups*. Boston, Mass.: Harvard Business School.

McDougall, W. (1923). *An Introduction to Social Psychology*. (15th. Edition) Boston: John W. Luce & Co.

McDougall, W. (1933). *The Energies of Men: A Study of the Fundamentals of Dynamic Psychology*. New York: Charles Scribner's Sons.

McDougall, W. (1964). The hormic psychology. In R. C. Tivan, & R. C. Birney (Eds.). *Theories of Motivation in Personality and Social Psychology*.

Mead, G. H. (1962). *Mind, Self, & Society from the Standpoint of a Social Behaviorist*. Chicago: The University of Chicago Press (first published 1934).

Mill, J. S. (2007). *On Liberty*. USA: Pearson Education (first published 1806).

Miller, M. (1984). *Plain Speaking: An Oral Biography of Harry S. Truman.* New York: The Berkley Publishing Group.

Montagu, A. (1978). *Touching: The Human Significance of the Skin.* New York: Harper & Row.

Moos, R. H. (1986). Work as a human context. In Pallak, M. S. and Perloff, R. O. (Eds.) (1986). *Psychology and Work: Productivity, Change, and Employment.* Washington, D. C.: American Psychological Association.

Osipow, S. H. (1986). Career issues through the life span. In Pallak, M. S., & Perloff, R. O. (Eds.). *Psychology and Work: Productivity, Change, and Employment.* Washington, D. C.: American Psychological Association.

Osmond, H. (1974). *Understanding Understanding.* New York: Bantam Books.

Pallak, M.S., & Perloff, R. O. (Eds.) (1986). *Psychology and Work: Productivity, Change, and Employment.* Washington, D. C.: American Psychological Association.

Pfeiffer, C. C. (Ed.) *Neurobiology of the Trace Metals Zinc and Copper.* NY: Academy Press, 1972.

Porter, L. W., Lawler III, E., & Hackman, J. R. Social influences on motivation. In Steers, R.M. & Porter, L. W. (1983). *Motivation and Work Behavior.* New York: McGraw-Hill, pp. 386–399.

Presthus, R. (1978). *The Organizational Society* (revised edition). New York: St. Martin's Press.

Rapoport, A. (1983). Technological models of the nervous system. *ETC. A Review of General Semantics,* Vol. 40, No. 3, 312–324.

Reagan, C. E. & Stewart, D. (Eds.) (1978). *The Philosophy of Paul Ricoeur: An Anthology of His Work.* Boston: Beacon Press.

Rees, F. (1991). *How to Lead Work Teams: Facilitation Skills.* San Diego: Pfeiffer & Co.

Reich, R. B. (1987). Entrepreneurship reconsidered: The team as hero. *Harvard Business Review.* 77–83.

Resnick, L. B., Levine, J. M. & Teasley, S. D. (Eds.) (1991). *Perspectives on Socially-Shared Cognition.* Washington, D. C.: American Psychological Association.

Ricoeur, P. (1994). *Oneself as Another* (transl. Kathleen Blamey). Chicago: The University of Chicago Press. Original Text: *Soi-même comme un autre.* Éditions du Seuil (1990).

Rue, L. W. and Byars, L. L. (1977). *Management: Theory and Application.* Homewood, IL.: Irwin.

Russell, B. (1993). *History of Western Philosophy.* London: Routledge (first published 1946).

Russell, B. (1996). *Authority and the Individual.* London: Routledge (first published 1949).

Safouan, M. (2003). *Speech or Death?* (transl. M. Thom). New York: Palgrave Macmillan.

Safouan, M. (2007). *Why are the Arabs not Free? — The Politics of Writing.* Oxford, UK: Blackwell Publishing.

Saïd, E. W. (1979). *Orientalism.* New York: Vintage.

Simon, H. A., *Administrative Behavior. A Study of Decision-making Processes in Administrative Organizations.* New York: The Free Press. Fourth edition.

Smelser, N. J., & Smelser, W. T. (1964). (Eds.) *Personality and Social Systems.* New York: Wiley.

Smith, T. V., & Greene, M. (Eds.) (1970). *From Descartes to Locke.* Chicago: The University of Chicago Press.

Steers, R.M. & Porter, L. W. (1983). *Motivation and Work Behavior.* New

York: McGraw-Hill. 386–399.

Straus, E. (1963). *The Primary World of Senses: A Vindication of Sensory Experience.* (transl. J. Needleman). New York: The Free Press of Glencoe.

Straus, E. (1982). *Man, Time, and World.* Pittsburgh, PA: Duquesne University Press. *The Type Reporter.* Vol. 1, No. 4. Spring 1985.

Sundstrom, E., De Meuse, K. P., & Futrell, D. (1990). Work teams: Applications and effectiveness. *American Psychologist, 45,* 2, 120-133.

Tornatzky, L. G. (1986). The psychology of self management in organizations. In Pallak, Varney, G. H. (1989). *Building Productive Teams: An Action Guide and Resource Book.* San Francisco: Jossey-Bass.

Verba, S. (1961). *Small Groups and Political Behavior — A Study of Leadership.* Princeton, N.J.: Princeton University Press.

Verba, S. (1961). *Leadership.* Princeton, N.J.: Princeton University Press.

Vickers, G. (1967). The multi-valued choice. In L. Thayer (Ed.), *Communication Concepts and Perspectives.* New York: Spartan Books.

Vico, G. (2001). *New Science: Principles of the New Science Concerning the Common Nature of Nations* (transl. D. March). Third Edition. London: Penguin Books.

Wittenbaum, G. M., & Moreland, R. L. (2008). Small-group research in social psychology: Topics and trends over time. *Social and Personality Psychology Compass* Vol. 2, No. 1, 187–203.

A p p e n d i x

※

FIGURE: 7

Social Structures

	Self	Individual	Group[1]	Public[2]	Nation	World	Universe
Individual	↰	↰	↰	↰	↰	↰	↰
Group							
Public							
Nation							
World							

[1]Group(s): small and large social systems.
[2]Public: profession, institution, neighborhood, socio-economic class *(generalized other)*.

Identification: Membership in any organization limits the member's freedom. In the meantime, it provides opportunities for growth and expression. There are aspects in one's personality that can be revealed in a social setting, namely away from the household. You are included in the organization through a group, never directly.

GROUP ANALYSIS FORM
By
A. Moneim El-Meligi

Rater's Name: _____   **Date**_____

Rater's Group: _____

INSTRUCTIONS

The purpose of this form is to draw your attention to the group as a living entity. To observe the group as such, you must avoid viewing individual members as separate entities. Focus instead on group processes such as interaction patterns; communications; roles individual members try to play; emergence of conflict and conflict resolution attempts; cooperative efforts; development of issues; participation; influence attempts and so on. Listed below are dimensions pertaining to group functioning. Each dimension is followed by five alternative descriptive statements. Decide which one of these statements best describes group functioning, then circle the number following this particular statement.

		SCORE
L.	**LEVEL OF ORGANIZATION**	
a.	completely disorganized	0
b.	loosely organized	1
c.	somewhat organized	2
d.	well organized	3
e.	very well organized	4
II.	**INVOLVEMENT IN GROUP ACTIVITY**	
a.	marked apathy throughout	0
b.	sporadic unenthusiastic participation	1
c.	occasional involvement on behalf of some members	2
d.	most members were moderately involved	3
e.	most members were genuinely involved throughout	4
III.	**TASK ASSUMPTION**	
a.	failed to initiate (or to adopt) a task	0
b.	mostly erratic about structuring (or defining) a task	1
c.	managed to initiate a task though in a vague manner	2
d.	somewhat successful in defining and agreeing upon a task	3
e.	markedly successful in assuming a well-defined task	4
IV.	**COOPERATION**	
a.	nobody seemed to care	0
b.	most of the burden fell on a small number of members	1
c.	only about half of the group assumed some responsibility	2
d.	responsibilities were distributed among the majority of members	3
e.	almost everybody in the group assumed a fair share of responsibility	4

2 of 2

V. DEVELOPMENT
    a. group ended where it started   0
    b. moved very little beyond the formulation of a task or objective   1
    c. was able to raise issues but fell short of reaching conclusions, solving
       problems, or achieving clear-cut goals   2
    d. somewhat successful in reaching conclusions, solving problems, or
       achieving clear-cut goals   3
    e. very successful outcome   4

VI. LEADERSHIP RESOURCES
    a. group lacked leadership throughout   0
    b. minimal or discontinuous assumption of leadership   1
    c. occasionally some members assumed leadership role   2
    d. one member (or several members) managed to lead the group fairly well   3
    e. all members cooperated so effectively that formal leadership was not needed   4

VII. GAINS
How much did you gain from being a participant in (or observer of) the group?
    a. nothing at all   0
    b. very little   1
    c. I gained some interesting information or ideas.   2
    d. provided me with a fresh look at some important issues   3
    e. I was very much enlightened and inspired   4

VIII. INTEREST
    To what extent did the group succeed in commanding your attention?
    a. I lost interest almost from the start   0
    b. I tried to listen (or watch) occasionally but my interest did not last   1
    c. I was somewhat interested in certain aspects (or individual contributions)   2
    d. I was interested more often than not   3
    e. I was absorbed in what was going on almost all the time   4

IX. ENJOYMENT
    How much did you enjoy being a participant (or observer of) the group?
    a. I definitely did not enjoy it   0
    b. I did not care one way or the other   1
    c. I enjoyed it with reservations   2
    d. I enjoyed it fairly well   3
    e. I thoroughly enjoyed it   4

ADD UP THE NUMBERS YOU HAVE CIRCLED AND ENTER THE TOTAL HERE _____

I ɳ d ℮ x

✳